ANNA K[...]

NOTES

including
- *Life of Tolstoy*
- *List of Characters*
- *Brief Synopsis of the Novel*
- *Chapter Summaries*
- *Critical Commentaries*
- *Analysis of Plot Structure*
- *Analysis of Tolstoy's Technique*
- *Analysis of the Novel's Themes*
- *Character Analyses*
- *Review Questions and Theme Topics*
- *Selected Bibliography*

by
Marianne Sturman

INCORPORATED

LINCOLN, NEBRASKA 68501

Editor	Consulting Editor
Gary Carey, M.A. *University of Colorado*	*James L. Roberts, Ph.D.* *Department of English* *University of Nebraska*

ISBN 0-8220-0183-7
© Copyright 1965
by
C. K. Hillegass
All Rights Reserved
Printed in U.S.A.

Cliffs Notes, Inc.   Lincoln, Nebraska

CONTENTS

THE LIFE OF LEO TOLSTOY (1828-1910)

Leo Nicolaevich Tolstoy was the next to youngest of five children, descending from one of the oldest and best families in Russia. His youthful surroundings were of the upper class gentry of the last period of serfdom. Though his life spanned the westernization of Russia, his early intellectual and cultural education was the traditional eighteenth century training. Lyovochka (as he was called) was a tender, affection seeking child who liked to do things "out of the ordinary." Self-consciousness was one of his youthful attributes and this process of self-scrutiny continued all his life. Indeed, Tolstoy's life is one of the best documented accounts we have of any writer, for the diaries he began at seventeen he continued through old age.

In 1844 Leo attended the University of Kazan, then one of the great seats of learning east of Berlin. He early showed a contempt for academic learning but became interested enough at the faculty of Jurisprudence (the easiest course of study) to attend classes with some regularity. Kazan, next to St. Petersburg and Moscow, was a great social center for the upper class. An eligible, titled young bachelor, Tolstoy devoted his energies to engage in the brilliant social life of his set. But his homely peasant face was a constant source of embarrassment and Tolstoy took refuge in queer and original behavior. His contemporaries called him "Lyovochka the bear," for he was always stiff and awkward.

Before his second year examinations, Tolstoy left Kazan to settle at his ancestral estate, Yasnaya Polyana (Bright Meadow) which was his share of the inheritance. Intending to farm and devote himself to improve the lot of his peasants, Tolstoy's youthful idealism soon vanished as he confronted the insurmountable distrust of the peasantry. He set off for Moscow in 1848 and for two years lived the irregular and dissipated life led by young men of his class. The diaries of this period reveal the critical self-scrutiny with which he regarded all his actions, and he itemized each deviation from his code of perfect behavior. Carnal lust and gambling were those passions most difficult for him to exorcise. As he closely observed the life around him in Moscow, Tolstoy experienced an irresistible urge to write. This time was the birth of the creative artist and the following year saw the publication of his first story, *Childhood*.

Tolstoy began his army career in 1852, joining his brother Nicolai in the Caucasus. Garrisoned among a string of Cossack outposts on the borders of Georgia, Tolstoy participated in occasional expeditions against the fierce Chechenians, the Tartar natives rebelling against Russian rule. He spent the rest of his time gambling, hunting, fornicating.

Torn amidst his inner struggle between his bad and good impulses, Tolstoy arrived at a sincere belief in God, though not in the formalized sense of the Eastern Church. The wild primitive environment of the Caucasus satisfied Tolstoy's intense physical and spiritual needs. Admiring the free, passionate, natural life of the mountain natives, he wished to turn his back forever on sophisticated society with its falseness and superficiality.

Soon after receiving his commission, Tolstoy fought among the defenders at Sevastopol against the Turks. In his *Sevastopol* sketches he describes with objectivity and compassion the matter-of-fact bravery of the Russian officers and soldiers during the siege.

By now he was a writer of nationwide reputation and when he resigned from the army and went to Petersburg, Turgenev offered him hospitality. With the leader of the capital's literary world for sponsor, Tolstoy became an intimate member of the circle of important writers and editors. But he failed to get on with these litterateurs: he had no respect for their ideal of European progress and their intellectual arrogance appalled him. His lifelong antagonism with Turgenev typified this relationship.

His travels abroad in 1857 started Tolstoy toward his lifelong revolt against the whole organization of modern civilization. To promote the growth of individual freedom and self-awareness, he started a unique village school at Yasnaya Polyana based on futuristic progressive principles. The peasant children "brought only themselves, their receptive natures, and the certainty that it would be as jolly in school today as yesterday." But the news of his brother's illness interrupted his work. Traveling to join Nicolai in France, he first made a tour of inspection throughout the German school system. He was at his brother's side when Nicolai died at the spa near Marseille, and this death affected him deeply. Only his work saved him from the worse depressions and sense of futility he felt toward life.

The fundamental aim of Tolstoy's nature was a search for truth, for the meaning of life, for the ultimate aims of art, for family happiness, for God. In marriage his soul found a release from this never ending quest, and once approaching his ideal of family happiness, Tolstoy entered upon the greatest creative period of his life.

In the first fifteen years of his marriage to Sonya (Sofya Andreyevna Bers) the great inner crisis he later experienced in his "conversion" was procrastinated, lulled by the triumph of spontaneous life over questioning reason. While his nine children grew up, his life was happy, almost idyllic, despite the differences which arose between him and the wife sixteen years his junior. As an inexperienced bride of eighteen, the city bred Sonya had many difficult adjustments to make. She was the mistress of a country estate as well as the helpmate of a man whose previous life she had not shared. Her constant pregnancies and boredom and loneliness marred the great love she and Tolstoy shared. In this exhilarating period of his growing family, Tolstoy created the epic novels, *War and Peace* and *Anna Karenina,* while Sonya, rejoicing at his creative genius, faithfully turned his rough drafts into fair copy.

Toward the end of 1866, while writing *Anna Karenina,* Tolstoy entered on the prolonged and fateful crisis which resulted in his conversion. He recorded part of this spiritual struggle in *Anna Karenina.* The meaning of life consists in living according to one's "inner goodness," he concluded. Only through emotional and religious commitment can one discover this natural truth. Uniquely interpreting the Gospels, Tolstoy discovered Christ's entire message was contained in the idea "that ye resist not evil." This doctrine of "non-resistance" became the foundation of Tolstoyism where one lived according to nature, renouncing the artificial refinements of society. Self-gratification, Tolstoy believed, perverted man's inherent goodness. Therefore property rights — ownership by one person of "things that belong to all" — is a chief source of evil. Carnal lust, ornamental clothing, fancy food are other symptoms of the corrupting influence of civilization. In accordance with his beliefs, Tolstoy renounced all copyrights to his works since 1881, divided his property among his family members, dressed in peasant homespun, ate only vegetables, gave up liquor and tobacco, engaged in manual work and even learned to cobble his own boots. Renouncing creative art for its corrupt refinements, Tolstoy wrote polemic tracts and short stories which embodied his new faith.

But the incongruity of his ideals and his actual environment grieved Tolstoy. With his family, he lived in affluence. His wife and children (except for Alexandra) disapproved of his philosophy. As they became more estranged and embittered from their differences, Sonya's increasing hysteria made his latter years a torment for Tolstoy.

All three stages of Tolstoy's life and writings (pre-conversion, conversion, effects of conversion) reflect the single quest of his career: to find the ultimate truth of human existence. After finding this truth, his life was a series of struggles to practice his preachings. He became a public figure both as a sage and an artist during his lifetime and Yasnaya Polyana became a mecca for a never-ceasing stream of pilgrims. The intensity and heroic scale of his life have been preserved for us from the memoirs of friends and family and wisdom seeking visitors. Though Tolstoy expressed his philosophy and theory of history with the same thoroughness and lucidity he devoted to his novels, he is known today chiefly for his important contributions to literature. Although his artistic influence is wide and still pervasive, few writers have achieved the personal stature with which to emulate his epic style.

MAIN CHARACTERS

Note: Every Russian has three names: first name, patronymic, last name. The root of the middle name is that of the father, plus a suffix meaning "son of" or "daughter of." Thus Anna's middle name is "Arkadyevna," while that of her brother is "Arkadyevitch." Russians call each other by the Christian name and patronymic, rarely by surname. For the sake of clarity, however, English translators use the characters' family names wherever possible.

Anna Arkadyevna Karenina
High society heroine whose love affair keynotes the novel.

Alexey Alexandrovitch Karenin
Anna's deceived husband. He is a frigid, lonely man with an influential government position in St. Petersburg.

Sergei Alexeyitch Karenin (Seriozha)
Anna's son whom she is forced to leave for her lover's sake.

Count Alexey Kirillovitch Vronsky
Anna's lover, an honorable, rich, handsome aide-de-camp with a promising army career which he gives up in order to live with Anna.

Konstantin Dmitrich Levin (Kostya)
Autobiographical hero of novel.

Princess Katerina Alexandrovna Shtcherbatsky (Kitty)
The eighteen year old debutante who becomes Levin's wife.

Prince Stepan Arkadyevitch Oblonsky (Stiva)
Anna's brother who is a pleasure-loving socialite.

Princess Darya Alexandrovna Oblonsky (Dolly)
Stiva's long-suffering wife and Kitty's older sister.

Nicolai Dmitrich Levin
   Levin's profligate brother who dies of tuberculosis.

Sergei Ivanitch Koznyshev
   Levin's elder half-brother who is a famous writer and intellectual.

SYNOPSIS OF *ANNA KARENINA*

PART 1 (34 chapters)

A crisis develops in the Oblonsky household when Dolly finds out about her husband's affair. Stiva's sister, Anna Karenina, arrives to reconcile the couple and dissuades Dolly from getting a divorce. Konstantin Levin, Stiva's friend, arrives in Moscow to propose to the eighteen year old Kitty Shtcherbatsky. She refuses him, for she loves Count Vronsky, a dashing army officer who has no intentions of marrying.

Meeting the lovely Madame Karenina, Vronsky falls in love and begins to pursue her. He and Anna are so involved with each other at the grand ball that Kitty's hopes for Vronsky are shattered. Anna, followed by Vronsky, returns to her husband and son in St. Petersburg, while the disappointed Levin returns to his country estate.

PART 2 (35 chapters)

Kitty falls ill after her humiliating rejection by Vronsky. At the German spa where she takes a rest cure she tries to deny her womanly nature by becoming a religious do-gooder. Realizing the hypocrisy of this new calling, Kitty returns to Russia cured of her depression and ready to accept her ultimate wifehood.

Consummating her union with Vronsky, Anna steps into a new life with much foreboding for the future. By the time she confesses her adultery to the suspecting Karenin, she is already pregnant with Vronsky's child.

PART 3 (32 chapters)

Devoting himself to farming, Levin tries to find life meaningful without marriage. He expends his energies in devising a cooperative landholding system with his peasants to make the best use of the land. Seeing his brother Nicolai hopelessly ill with tuberculosis, he realizes he has been working to avoid facing the problem of death. He also realizes he will always love Kitty.

Vronsky's career ambitions rival his love, and as he has not chosen between them, he is still uncommitted to Anna. Having rejected her husband, but still unable to depend on Vronsky, Anna finds her situation desperate. Her life is in a state of suspension.

PART 4 (23 chapters)

Kitty and Levin are engaged to marry. Karenin, who has tried to maintain appearances of domestic tranquillity, finally builds up enough anger to hire a divorce lawyer. Anna is confined of a daughter, but dangerously ill from puerperal fever. At her deathbed, Karenin forgives her and feels sanctified by this surge of humanity and Christian charity. At this sudden reversal of their roles Vronsky feels so humiliated he attempts suicide. These incidents form the turning point of the novel. After Anna's recovery, the lovers go abroad and Anna refuses divorce (though Karenin agrees to it) for fear of giving up her son.

PART 5 (33 chapters)

Levin and Kitty, after some initial difficulties, adjust to being married. Nicolai's death affects Levin deeply, and he realizes that emotional commitment, not reason, enables one to overcome life's problems. As if to underscore his life-affirmation, they learn Kitty is pregnant.

After they honeymoon in Italy, Anna and Vronsky return to Petersburg. Violently affected from seeing her son again, Anna's love for Vronsky becomes more desperate now that she has no one else. Despite his objections, she boldly attends the theater as if to affirm her love before conventional society. Humiliated at the opera, she blames Vronsky for lacking sympathy with her suffering, while he is angry at her indiscretion. This keynotes the decline of their relationship, although it is temporarily restored as they go to live in the country.

PART 6 (32 chapters)

Among Levin's summer visitors is a socialite who pays so much attention to Kitty that Levin asks him to leave. Visiting Anna at Vronsky's estate, Dolly finds her own drab life preferable to the formal luxury and decadence of Anna's. Complaining that Vronsky is eager for independence, Anna tells Dolly she must rely on her beauty and her love to keep his interest. Vronsky feels especially burdened by the demands of Anna's love when she calls him home from a refreshing political convention.

PART 7 (31 chapters)

Kitty gives birth to a son. Karenin, under the influence of his fanatically devout friend, Countess Lydia Ivanovna, becomes religious and uses his hypocritical faith as a crutch to overcome his humiliation and loneliness.

Anna, seeing the irreversible decline of her love affair, has no more will to live and commits suicide.

PART 8 (19 chapters)

Vronsky volunteers for service in the Russo-Turkish war. Tolstoy uses this part of the novel to express his pacifist principles. Levin discovers "salvation" when he resolves to "live for his soul" rather than for selfish goals. He realizes the meaning of life consists in living according to the goodness inherent in every individual. Understanding death as part of a reality-oriented life, Levin is at peace with himself.

PART 1

CHAPTERS 1 to 5

Summary
The household of Prince Stepan Arkadyevitch Oblonsky is in a state of confusion that began three days ago when his wife discovered his relationship with their former French governess. Dolly Oblonsky says she can no longer live in the same house with her husband.

Stiva (as he is called) considers her attitude unnecessarily harsh, despite the gravity of the situation. Though she is a good mother to their five children and manages the household well, she is worn out and no longer young or good looking; whereas he feels himself in prime enjoyment of his powers. Meanwhile all the servants, painfully aware of the Oblonsky's problems, feel a separation is imminent.

On the third day, while the barber shaves his face, Stiva reads a telegram, announcing that his sister, Anna Arkadyevna Karenina, will arrive tomorrow to visit. Perhaps she might reconcile husband and wife.

Dressed and shaved, feeling fragrant and comfortable, Stepan Arkadyevitch reads his letters, some office papers, and peruses a liberal newspaper, one advocating the views of the liberal majority and satisfying to his truthful temperament. Interrupting his reading, he affectionately greets two of his children, treating them to bon-bons as he sends them off.

While his carriage awaits him, Stiva sees a petitioner and gives her advice. Taking his hat, he feels as if he forgot something. Lighting a cigarette, squaring his shoulders, he rapidly walks to his wife's bedroom.

Darya Alexandrovna is collecting her things and the children's clothes in order to pack up and leave for her mother's house. Regarding her husband out of startled eyes, prominent in her sunken and thin face, she scans his figure which radiates health and freshness. Though he tries to look pitiful and humble, she notes with disgust that good nature of his which everyone praises and likes so well.

The brief interview fails. Dolly shrilly insists she will leave the house, while Stiva pleads his guilt and begs her to forgive his one lapse of passion which could not belie their nine years of happy marriage. When he weeps in sympathy for her, Dolly becomes angrier than ever: she seeks his love, not his pity.

Dolly leaves the room to attend to a child crying in the nursery. Plunging into the duties of the day, she crowds the grief out of her mind for a time. Stiva slowly leaves the room. "Maybe she will come around," he tells himself.

Commentary

"Happy families are all alike," Tolstoy writes as the first words of *Anna Karenina,* "Every unhappy family is unhappy in its own way." Specifying this generalization the author details the life of a well favored aristocrat. Stepan Arkadyevitch has an excellent post in Moscow, is the head of a loving and smoothly run household. His wife, Darya, Stiva's feminine counterpart in the Russian class system, centers her life on raising the children and tending her husband. But his infidelity shatters their harmonious life and Dolly must confront the problem of how to repair her personal ruin. For Stiva, his marital life is of secondary value; his official duties, his social activities, and his pleasures are primary. Thus we see that the values of men and women in this society are oriented toward different goals and Stiva's affair with the French governess causes these different values to stand in clear relief.

In these chapters Tolstoy has set up a small working model which generates all the subsequent themes of *Anna Karenina.* Stiva's petty love affair prefigures the adultery of Anna with Vronsky, and serves as a negative comparison with Levin's successful marriage later in the novel. The individual's quest for meaning through personal relationships and through the details of ordinary life begins — though modestly — among the descriptions of domestic life in the Oblonsky household.

CHAPTERS 6 to 11

Summary

Stepan Arkadyevitch, one who "was born in the midst of those who has been and are the powerful ones of this world" is president of a government board in Moscow, part of a department in the ministry where his brother-in-law, Alexey Alexandrovitch Karenin, holds one of the most prominent positions. Stiva's kindliness and good humor have won him the respect and liking of all his subordinates as well as his superiors. Despite excellent abilities, Stiva did poorly at school for he was idle and mischievous. Yet he does a good job at the office; never getting carried away with his work, his indifference to the business at hand increases his objectivity and accuracy.

During his busy morning, Stiva receives the unexpected visit of his childhood comrade, Konstantin Levin, an intense, thoughtful man of the same age. Levin, modeled after Tolstoy himself, cares deeply for farming, raising livestock, and managing his ancestral estate. He despises town life for being superficial and frivolous, while Stiva considers Levin's affairs as trifling. Despite their differences, the two men have remained close friends. Levin's love for Dolly's youngest sister, Kitty Shtcherbatsky, also reinforces their friendship.

Konstantin Dmitrievitch Levin has come to Moscow specifically to make an offer to the Princess Shtcherbatsky. He regards Kitty as a perfect creature and feels unworthy beside her. Though he believes she deserved better than an ugly, ordinary man like himself, he feels he could not have a moment's rest until he made her an offer.

When Levin arrives at Moscow, he puts up at the house of his elder half-brother, Koznyshev. Sergey Ivanitch Koznyshev, a famous thinker and writer, concerned with intellectual problems and immersing himself in the political trends of Russia, is of an entirely different temperament than Levin. Rather than ask his brother's advice on his personal problem, Levin tells Koznyshev of his disenchantment with his local Zemstvo organization and they talk about provincial self-government in general. (Zemstvos are representative county councils founded in 1864 by Alexander II.)

Sergey Ivanitch remarks that their brother Nicolai had turned up in Moscow and shows Levin a hostile note he received. Nicolai, after Koznyshev had covered an I.O.U. for him, writes that the only favors he wishes of his brothers is that they leave him in peace. Half-brother to Koznyshev, and elder brother to Konstantin, Nicolai has dissipated the greater part of his fortune, quarrelled with his brothers, and lives in the strangest and lowest company. Levin at once wants to visit his ruined brother, but first drives to the place where he might meet Kitty.

Arriving at the Zoological gardens' skating rink, Kitty's presence dominates his thoughts and he sees no one but her. The expression of her eyes — soft, serene, thoughtful — and her smile transports him and he feels softened and tender as in his early childhood. An excellent skater, Levin works off some of his nervousness by executing a daring leap down the coffee house steps. While he and Kitty skate together, Levin responds so meaningfully to her casual questions that he constantly blushes. She asks how long he intends to stay in Moscow. "It depends on you," Levin says, and is horrorstruck at his inadvertent confession. Kitty stumbles, then hurries away from him toward her parents. Her mother, having higher hopes for her child, gives Levin a cold greeting but invites him to call on them. To offset her mother's coolness, Kitty bids him a friendly farewell and her smile throws Levin into ecstasy.

Stiva now arrives. After greeting his in-laws, he draws Levin off to dinner, intently planning their menu while they drive to the restaurant. Oblonsky is perfectly at home among the bronzes, starchy tablecloths, mirrors, obsequious waiters. In their private dining room, he selects their wines and courses with elaborate care. Levin feels almost sullied in this luxurious atmosphere. After the freshness of skating and his delight in the innocence and truthfulness of Kitty, his present setting seems stale and artificial. People in the country, he tells Stiva, order their lives around the goal of work, not idleness. City people, having lost touch with the functional aspects of life, are only prepared to seek pleasure. "Why yes," answers Stiva good-naturedly, "That's just the aim of civilization — to make everything a source of pleasure." Oblonsky, guessing why Levin returned to Moscow, declares he would be delighted to have him as a brother-in-law. He wonders if Levin knows Count Vronsky, for this handsome aide-de-camp is also in love with Kitty. Alexey Kirillovitch Vronsky, rich, brilliant, and well connected, is, according to Stiva "one of the finest specimens of the gilded youth of Petersburg." Levin pales at this news. He feels that Stiva's counsels and talk of rivalry profane his great feeling for Kitty.

Oblonsky tells Levin of his own domestic problems and Konstantin cannot understand that a man would go "straight to the bakeshop and steal a roll" when he has just dined on plenty. Fiercely monogamous, Levin says he has "a loathing for fallen women" but then recollects his own sins. Stiva points out that life does not consist of clear-cut principles; its variety, charm, and beauty is made up of "light and shadow" and that Levin is wrong to believe that one's work, one's relationships, one's thoughts must always correspond to a defined aim in life.

After dinner, the two friends part. Levin looks forward to his evening at the Shtcherbatskys where his fate will be decided.

Commentary

Levin enters the novel in a customary outburst of frankness and intense conviction. He tells Stiva he no longer participates in the Zemstvo, derides Oblonsky's bureaucratic job as a sinecure, and mentions Kitty, Immediately we learn of his main impulses: his quest for rural reform, his rejection of town life, and his passion for Kitty. Levin's character becomes further defined by a comparison to that of Koznyshev and Nicolai, and during his behavior in the episodes at the skating rink. The discussion between Levin and Stiva as they dine concentrates other themes of *Anna Karenina* which Tolstoy later defines, especially that of the conflict between monogamy and sexual freedom. Defending the undivided family, Levin cuts himself short as he recalls his own lapses. This moment keynotes the inconsistencies between personal ideals and personal behavior, a problem which Levin (and Tolstoy) struggles with and a problem which Stiva overlooks and rationalizes by his hedonism.

CHAPTERS 12 to 15

Summary

Tolstoy introduces Kitty, the eighteen-year-old girl, who was spending her first winter "out in the world" and who already has two serious suitors, Levin and Count Vronsky. Kitty's parents, having gone through the anxieties of getting their two elder daughters married off, have renewed arguments over their third. The old Princess Shtcherbatsky reflects how much easier it was in the older days when young girls did not demand their own freedom of choice in marriage. Nowadays it is hard for parents to know when to use their influence to protect their daughters against a rash or unsuccessful choice. The old prince prefers Levin for his plainness and honesty, while his wife prefers Vronsky for his dash and brilliance. She wonders why the young officer, openly flirting with Kitty at balls and calling on her at home, has not yet made an offer.

Kitty considers her feelings toward each of her suitors. While she feels "perfectly simple and clear" with Levin and somewhat awkward with Vronsky, she decides she prefers the dashing officer.

Kitty receives Levin in the drawing-room alone. He blurts out his proposal, his heart sinking as he gazes at her. "That cannot be," Kitty whispers, "Forgive me." The old princess arrives and guesses what has happened; pleased, she welcomes Levin cordially.

Vronsky arrives among the other guests, and Levin remains to see the man Kitty loves. He sees Vronsky as an agreeable, sincere, very calm and intelligent person. Levin soon finds an opportunity to slip quietly away.

As she gets ready for sleep, Kitty rehearses the events of the evening. Though elated at having received an offer, she weeps as she recalls Levin's kind eyes filled with dejection. Downstairs her parents argue. The old prince accuses his wife of debasing their child by catching "an eligible gentleman" for her and discouraging her feelings for Levin, by far the better man. If Kitty falls in love with Vronsky, a "peacock" and featherhead "who's only amusing himself," she might meet the same fate as their unfortunate Dolly.

Commentary

Kitty, although ready to love, is still not mature enough to discriminate. But she is flooded with happiness at Levin's proposal and does not know why. Vronsky is introduced in the most favorable way, and, at Kitty's unfeigned joy at his arrival, the theme of her indiscriminate love deepens.

As Kitty's mother reflects on the simpleness of matchmaking when she was a girl, Tolstoy telescopes the family history through his characteristic device of "interior monologue." This discussion also pinpoints a primary theme of the novel — the problem of marriage in a modern society.

CHAPTERS 16 to 23

Summary

Vronsky, after his luxurious and coarse life in Petersburg, finds a "great and delicate pleasure" in the affection of this "sweet and innocent girl," though he feels no urge to marry and sees nothing wrong in paying attention to Kitty. The next day, waiting at the train station to meet his mother, he meets Oblonsky, whose sister is arriving on the same train. When Stiva explains that Levin's depressed mood last night was the result of Kitty's refusal, Vronsky feels like a conqueror and a hero.

When the train arrives, his mother introduces him to her traveling companion, the charming Madame Karenina; something peculiarly "caressing and soft" in the expression of her face catches his attention. Countess

Vronsky explains this is the first time Anna has been away from her eight year old child and is somewhat anxious. "Yes," Anna smiles, "the countess and I have been talking all the time, I of my son and she of hers." Vronsky unable to take his eyes from Madame Karenina watches her walk lightly and rapidly with her brother to their carriage, carrying her "rather full figure with extraordinary lightness."

A sudden accident at the station draws a crowd. A guard, not hearing the train move back, has been crushed under the wheels of the car. Anna is horrified and even more impressed to learn that the man is the only support of an immense family. "Couldn't something be done?" she asks, and learns a few moments later that Vronsky had given 200 rubles for the benefit of the widow. Suspecting that this gesture has something to do with her, Anna frowns; it is something that ought not to have been.

In the carriage, Stiva wonders at her quivering lips and her tears. "It's an omen of evil," Anna says, and changes the subject. "Have you known Vronsky long?" she asks. "Yes," answers Stiva, "We're hoping he will marry Kitty." "Indeed?" says Anna softly, then with a toss of her head, "Come, let's talk about you and what you wrote me about in your letter."

Anna's kindness and warmth, as well as her accurate recollection of the names, ages, and past illnesses of the Oblonsky children win Dolly's confidence. Eventually Anna talks of the problem that brought her to Moscow in the first place. She points out how miserable Stiva felt at his infidelity and how repentant he is. "I don't know how much love there still is in your heart for him," she tells Dolly. "You alone know whether there is enough for you to be able to forgive. If there is, then forgive him!" Dolly won over by Anna's sympathy and understanding, feels much comforted.

Kitty calls on the following day, soon finding herself in love with Anna, "as young girls often fall in love with older and married women." Anna's eagerness, freshness, and the elasticity of her movements seem to be those of a girl in her twenties, while her seriousness and mournful smile attract Kitty to her maturity. Congratulating Kitty on behalf of Vronsky, Anna relates an incident where the young man had saved a woman from drowning, a story told her by Countess Vronsky. But she does not mention the incident of the 200 rubles; fearing something personal in that gesture, she does not like to think of it. Dolly's children, shrieking with delight to see their aunt, interrupt further conversation, while Anna runs laughing to meet them. After dinner, Vronsky unexpectedly passes by but declines to join them. Kitty assumes he comes to seek her but does not wish to intrude while they have a guest. The visit seems odd to all of them, but particularly to Anna and she is troubled.

The great ball is held the following evening, and Kitty, intoxicated by the elegance of gowns around her, the lighted chandeliers, the liveried footmen, feels her eyes sparkle and her lips rosy as young men constantly ask her to dance. She is certain that Count Vronsky will propose to her this night. Anna appears, beautifully elegant in a simple low-cut black velvet gown that brings out all her charm. Elated to see Vronsky, Kitty wonders why Anna deliberately refrains from answering his bow of greeting. Vronsky tells Kitty he has regretted not seeing her for so long. As they face each other during the pause before the dance, Kitty gives him a look "so full of love—that look, which met with no response, pierced her heart with unending shame for years after." During her quadrille with another partner, Kitty observes Anna and Vronsky dancing opposite. On Anna's expressive face appears the signs of excitement and success that she herself feels familiar with, while Vronsky's expression, always firm and independent, bears a look of "bewilderment and humbled submissiveness, like the expression of an intelligent dog when it has done wrong." Kitty's world crumbles; only her self-discipline allows her to continue dancing and smiling and talking.

Commentary

We first hear of Anna Karenina in Chapter 1, where she intends to arrive at Moscow to repair a broken marriage: indeed an ironic touch on the part of the author. The railroad station, the scene of Anna's first meeting with Vronsky, provides a symbol that concentrates the ideas of beginning, and, representing a point of departure as well. Alighting in Moscow, Anna confronts a new destiny and enters a foreign world. The "evil omen" which makes her shudder foreshadows her doom.

What is outstanding in Anna is her charm and fascination, apparent to Vronsky as their glances first meet. Capable of deep and strong passions, her whole being is directed toward love. Tolstoy writing that "her whole nature was so brimming over with something that against her will it showed itself..." indicates that her capacity for love has not yet been awakened.

Another outstanding quality is Anna's maturity. When she tells Vronsky that she and his mother have talked about their sons throughout the journey, Anna assumes herself a generation older than her future lover. This "age" difference between them underscores the essential duplicity and futility of their future relationship. The comparison of Seriozha with Vronsky also foreshadows Anna's later dilemma when she must choose between her child and her lover.

Anna becomes the object of fascination and love for everyone in her brother's household. She appeals to the children, wins Dolly's confidence; Kitty falls in love with her for her qualities of youth (denoting her peerage and future competition with Kitty) and maturity (denoting the emotional depth which charms Vronsky). But her charm is "diabolical and strange" at the same time. Kitty notices this during the ball when Anna regards her smilingly and with "drooping eyelids."

The key to Anna's personality and the quality which endears her to Tolstoy is her naturalness and emotional depth. She responds with her heart, not with applying social principles. Counseling Dolly to forgive Stiva, Anna argues, not from the standpoint of maintaining appearances to preserve a reputation before society, but from inner emotions. If you love him, then forgive him, Anna says. At the same time this quality provides the source of Anna's nobility, it also increases her susceptibility for a lawless passion.

In these episodes which reveal subtleties of individual character and relationships, a few of Tolstoy's narrative devices deserve brief mention. Though he is thoroughly an omniscient author, Tolstoy allows us to view the ball through the narrower — and more intense — viewpoint of Kitty, who watches Vronsky fall under Anna's spell. Kitty's suffering conveys to us the full quality of Madame Karenina's fascination.

Tolstoy also shows great dexterity in handling the psychological tensions and their physical relief. A good example of this occurs when Anna tells Kitty what a chivalrous nature Vronsky has. She relates how he saved a woman from drowning but refrains from mentioning the incident of the 200 rubles. In the pause, her frown keynotes the deceit which will enmesh her more and more; but at that moment, the children rush in and Anna, laughing, tumbles them to the ground.

CHAPTERS 24 to 27

Summary

Leaving the Shtcherbatskys, Levin walks to his brother's lodgings. He thinks how worthless he is, and Kitty is right to prefer Vronsky. He thinks of the ugliness of his brother's life, and how unfair it is for society to judge his outward achievements when his soul is as truthful and as full of goodness as anyone else's.

Thin and emaciated from consumption, Nicolai lives in squalor with his common-law wife, Marya Nicolaevna (Masha), whom he had rescued from a brothel. Finding his brother demoralized by illness, drunkenness, and a life of failure. Levin is too depressed to stay long. He has Masha promise to write him in case of need and takes the first train home, arriving toward evening of the next day.

Catching sight of his waiting coachman at the station, receiving the news of his estate—a cow had calved, the contractor had arrived—Levin feels his confusion and despondency drop away. He resolves to always help his brother, to abandon his dreams of happiness through marriage, and never give way to low passions, memories of which now torture him with unassuageable guilt. Like Dolly caught up in her household, the management of his large estate absorbs Levin's thoughts and temporarily soothes his disappointment.

His house represents his whole world, for here his parents spent their lives and here he and his brother were born. Although his mother died when he was very young, her image is sacred to him, and his future wife must satisfy the holy ideal of woman he conceives in his mother's image. Unlike his friends for whom marriage is merely one of the numerous facts of social life, Levin considers it the chief affair of life, basic to his entire happiness. He has always looked forward to the family he would have, then, secondarily, to the wife.

Sipping a cup of tea that evening, sitting with his faithful housekeeper, Agafea Mihalovna, reading a book, Levin daydreams. He finds all nature in unity and at peace. "One must struggle to live better, much better," he muses, happily concluding that "nothing's amiss, all's well."

Commentary
These chapters show Levin in his true element. His house, his land, his peasants represent his roots and the source of his nourishment. The happiness Levin feels upon returning to his estate after the suffering experienced in Moscow prefigures the salvation he finds at the end of the novel. Moreover, Levin's return to the country strikes a strong contrast with the events at the ball. This section emphasizes the thematic duality of the novel which unfolds more and more in subsequent parts: Anna and Vronsky and the social milieu of town life, Levin and Kitty and the natural life of the country.

CHAPTERS 28 to 33

Summary
Anna wants to leave Moscow the next day. Dolly finds her sister-in-law strangely nervous, always close to tears, but Anna is unable to tell

her why, that she is leaving sooner than intended in order to avoid Vronsky. She confesses to Dolly that Kitty is jealous on her account and she had caused her misery at the ball. Dolly remonstrates soothingly, saying she is glad that her sister had no further hopes for Vronsky since he is so fickle. At parting the two women embrace and profess sincere affection.

Nervous and excited, Anna is relieved to be on the train journeying home to her son and husband and resume her nice comfortable way of life again. She thinks of Vronsky and wonders at her vague feeling of shame when there is nothing to be ashamed about. Still tense, she alights at the next station for a breath of cold air. Suddenly Vronsky appears at her side and she is seized by a feeling of joyful pride at his look of reverence and devotion. "You know that I have come to be where you are," he says, "I can't help it." Pausing before her answer, Anna feels this moment in the midst of a snowstorm has drawn them close together. She begs him to forget, as she had forgotten it, the statement he has just uttered.

Still in her tense mood, Anna cannot sleep for the rest of the trip. Meeting her husband at the station, she feels dissatisfied with "his imposing and frigid figure, his high pitched voice, now noticing how his ears stick out. What she suddenly recognizes for the first time, is "an intimate feeling, like a consciousness of hypocrisy, which she experienced in her relations with her husband."

As her son dashes downstairs to greet her at home she feels that even he is somewhat less delightful in reality than in the image she had of him while away. But her pleasure in his caresses, seeing his plump little shape, his curls and blue eyes soothes her. After a visit from Karenin's friend, the Countess Lydia Ivanovna, and after unpacking and dining with her son, Anna feels resolute and irreproachable as she assumes the habitual conditions of her life.

Karenin appears for dinner precisely at five o'clock, and leaves for a meeting afterwards. Every minute of his life is portioned out and occupied, for Karenin adheres to the strictest punctuality in order to accomplish what he requires himself to do. "Unhasting and unresting" is his motto.

When Alexey Alexandrovitch returns, at exactly half past nine, Anna chats with him, recounting everything about her visit to Moscow while refraining from mentioning Vronsky. Karenin flatly denounces Oblonsky's extra-marital dalliance, and Anna thinks what a truthful, good-hearted man her husband is. In her thoughts she defends him as if someone said he is someone she cannot love.

Commentary

Anna's journey back to her home represents her retreat from the emotional stimulation she experienced through Vronsky. Her attempt at flight, however, is interrupted by the presence of the young officer who takes the same train. The snowstorm in which they meet corresponds to the stormy state of their emotions.

Anna's suddenly perceived dissatisfaction with her husband's appearance and manner, and her slight disappointment upon first seeing her son, shows her perceptions of the life she has been familiar with have already been changed under the influence of this passion to which she is still unawakened. But her feverish state passes when she reassumes her old habits and the "causeless shame" she felt during her journey vanishes.

The character of Karenin, with its compulsiveness and dullness, shows that he is a poor foil for Anna's vivacity and love of life. Tolstoy also shows their relationship is routine and erotically incomplete as "precisely at twelve o'clock," Karenin bids Anna to bed. She follows, "but her face had none of the eagerness which, [in Moscow] fairly flashed from her eyes and her smile; on the contrary, now the fire seemed quenched in her, hidden somewhere far away."

CHAPTER 34

Summary

Vronsky returns to his Petersburg apartment and finds his favorite comrade, Petrivsky, there with some friends, including Baroness Shilton, Petrivsky's current companion. Amidst the slightly drunken chatter and gossip of his gay, broad-minded companions, Vronsky drops back into the light-hearted pleasant world he has always lived in. He has a bantering discussion with Baroness Shilton about divorce. Her husband, she says, wants to keep her property by way of retribution for her unfaithfulness.

Vronsky dresses himself in his uniform to report to his regiment. He plans, among other visits, to pay his cousin Princess Betsy Tverskoy a call. Related to Anna through marriage, Betsy would bring him into that society where he might meet Madame Karenina. As he always does in Petersburg, Vronsky leaves home, not meaning to return until late at night.

Commentary

In this chapter Vronsky returns to his familiar habits, just as Dolly, Levin, and Anna have gone back to their "starting points" after confronting their respective crises. Vronsky's light talk with the baroness about divorce preludes his more intense arguments with Anna later on, and the behavior attributed to Baron Shilton suggests the nature of Karenin's response to the same problem.

Part 1 ends on a note of departure, as Vronsky leaves to form connections which will give him further chances to see Anna. This lightly undertaken departure, however, represents one with grave consequences for Vronsky: he is really departing from his old way of life with its facile relationships to embark upon a new existence and a relationship of unimagined intensity.

PART 2

CHAPTERS 1 to 3

Summary
Kitty is ill, and the prominent specialist who examines her, finding nothing specifically wrong suggests she be taken abroad to a health spa. Her father and Dolly both realize that Kitty's nervous irritability is due to a broken heart. The old prince blames his wife for influencing Kitty's affections in the first place, while Dolly explains to her mother that Kitty had refused Levin whom she might have accepted had she not counted on Vronsky's proposal. Princess Shtcherbatsky finally realizes the sin she committed against her daughter.

Tearful and miserable when Dolly comes to her room, Kitty does not divulge what her sister has already guessed: that she is ready to love and accept Levin and detest Vronsky. Instead Kitty rages. She says she is ashamed and humiliated at discovering herself to be a marketable commodity, that all the eligible men are free to look her over, that her parents are only interested in marrying her off. She only feels free with Dolly and the children, Kitty says.

Dolly's difficulties at that time were no better. Besides suspecting further infidelities of Stiva, Dolly is always short of money and her large family is a constant source of worry. Besides a new baby in the house, Dolly has to care for the children ill with scarlet fever. Kitty goes home with her sister to nurse the youngsters through their illnesses, and still unwell six weeks later, she and her parents go abroad during Lent.

Commentary
Kitty's first venture into womanhood, resulting in failure, makes her retreat back into a dependence on her family. Having suffered deep humiliation on the very occasion she was intoxicated by her attractiveness and

femininity (the moment when she looked with love at Vronsky) her reaction is to deny her womanhood. Kitty's physical illness expresses the violence of her denial. Kitty's immaturity is shown by her choice of Vronsky over Levin; still influenced by her mother, she lacks the self-knowledge which would prompt her to choose accurately.

Kitty's crisis confuses her mother's sense of duty. While realizing she was wrong to influence her child, Princess Shtcherbatsky feels it is wrong not to guide her daughter. Besides touching on the difficulty of communication between generations, Tolstoy shows that judgments based on social principles rather than emotional values lead to disappointment and disillusion.

CHAPTERS 4 to 11

Summary

Three social spheres form subdivisions of Petersburg's top society: one is composed of Karenin's government officials, another that of elderly, benevolent, pious women and their learned, ambitious husbands. Centered around the Countess Lydia Ivanovna, and called the "conscience of St. Petersburg", this set is the one through which Karenin built his career and the one Anna has been closely connected with. Of late, feeling bored and ill at ease in this group whom she suspects of hypocrisy, Anna prefers the third circle of society proper—the world of balls and dinner parties. Her link with this group is through the Princess Betsy Tverskoy. In this circle, Anna and Vronsky frequently meet.

At one of Betsy's dinner parties, they are engrossed in talk. Anna begs him, if he loves her as he says, to leave her in peace. But Vronsky, his face radiant as he pleads his love, says it is impossible for him to live separately from her. Anna is unable to reply. As she looks into his face with eyes full of love, Vronsky is ecstatic.

Karenin arrives, and glancing toward his wife in her animated conversation with Vronsky, talks with Betsy. While seeing nothing improper or peculiar in his wife's behavior, Karenin notices the disapproval of the other guests. Leaving before dinner, though Anna insists to remain, Alexey Alexandrovitch resolves to mention the matter this evening.

Thinking it over, Karenin decides a talk is not such a simple matter after all. For the first time he tries to imagine what his wife thinks and feels, whether she could possibly stop loving him and turn to another man. The irrational and illogical feeling of jealousy throws him into confusion. Having always lived for his work in official spheres — a reflection of life — Karenin is horrified to suddenly confront life itself. While composing the speech he would deliver to Anna, he tries to soothe himself. But the sound of a carriage driving up, then the sound of her light step on the stairs, frightens him.

Anna pretends surprise at his request for a talk. Inwardly marvelling at her confident answers, she feels herself clad in an impenetrable armor of falsehood and wonders how easily she can lie. Karenin notices the change immediately. The depths of her soul, always open to him before, now close against him. Looking into her laughing eyes, alarming with their impenetrability, Karenin feels the utter uselessness and idleness of his words.

He warns that her thoughtlessness and indiscretion might cause herself to be spoken of in society, her "too animated conversation" with Count Vronsky this evening which attracted attention, to give an example. Anna responds cheerfully and seems sincere. Reminding her of her duty, for their lives have been joined "not by man but by God" Karenin says this concerns not himself, but Anna and their son. "I have nothing to say," she answers, restraining a smile, "and it really is bed-time."

Their talk marks a new life for Karenin and his wife. Though outwardly unchanged, their intimate relations completely alter. Forceful when dealing with affairs of state, Karenin feels helpless dealing with his wife. "Like an ox with bent head" he waits submissively for the axe which he feels raised above him.

Vronsky satisfies his one desire which absorbed him for nearly a year. Overcome by her sense of degradation, Anna sobs and does not speak. Her shame infects him, and he feels a "murderer's horror before the body of his victim." Realizing "the murderer must make use of what he has obtained by his crime" Anna sadly submits to his kisses for "these are what have been bought by my shame." "Everything is over," she says, "I have nothing but you left. Remember that."

The shame, rapture, and horror she feels upon stepping into a new life drives all other feelings from her. She has no calm left in which to reflect on what occurred, but in her dreams she has to face her ugly position. She dreams she is the wife of Alexey Alexandrovitch as well as of Alexey Vronsky. As both caress her, she explains to them, laughing, that what had seemed impossible before is now simply and satisfactorily arranged. Both men are contented and happy. Anna's dream is like a nightmare and she awakes from it in terror.

Commentary

Anna's awakening passion changes the pattern of her social life. She avoids the serious group because its members are hypocrites, and attends the brilliant functions of Betsy's set. Her sudden awareness of hypocrisy reflects her awareness of her own deceit. This deceit, however, is two fold. Anna suspects that her emotionally incomplete existence as the faithful wife of a man she realizes now she does not love was basically hypocritical. The other source of deceit is adultery, a condition of fraud defined by society. At the same time, adultery provides the only means by which Anna can redeem her false marriage: through Vronsky she can achieve a truthful love relationship. This conflict between emotional truth and formal truth is the basis of Anna's tragedy.

At the point of Karenin's talk with Anna, however, there is no conflict. While her husband points out the social consequences of "indiscretion" and "tactless behavior," Anna can barely suppress a smile. Social convention, her smile says, is a trivial matter compared with emotional values, and her feelings for Karenin are trivial compared with her passion for Vronsky.

The tragic consequences of "stepping into a new life" suddenly loom large and real when Anna and Vronsky consummate their relationship. A life with two husbands is that of an outlaw; having broken one of the most forceful social conventions, Anna denies herself the protection society offers. She has no one left but her "accomplice."

Vronsky's position is less serious than Anna's, and he has pursued his conquest with more frivolous intentions. Though his love is deep — deeper than he realizes — his officers' code of behavior sets a prestige value on seducing married women: the higher her social standing, the higher the man's prestige. Tolstoy shows Vronsky's awareness of these values as Betsy and her cousin chat during intermission at the opera.

Only when he sees Anna's shame and when she rejects his platitudes about "moment of happiness" does Vronsky gain insight into the seriousness of his crime against her. Tolstoy's analogy of a murderer and his victim underscores the extent of Vronsky's commitment to Anna and forecasts her doom and his culpability.

CHAPTERS 12 to 17

Summary

In the early days of his return to the country Levin suffers deeply. Gradually the bitter memory of his rejection disappears as the daily incidents of his country life absorb him. With the coming of spring and his plans for many improvements on his estate, he is quite happy.

Stepan Arkadyevitch appears one evening for he is to sell a forest on his wife's property nearby. Stiva and Levin enjoy an excellent day of stand-shooting, returning with a good catch of snipe. While Oblonsky and the prospective purchaser, Ryabinin, haggle over the price of the forest, Levin fumes. Stiva, hungry for cash, settles for a much lower price than Konstantin thinks the property is worth.

Later on, the two friends talk of the Shtcherbatskys, and Levin learns of Kitty's illness, of Vronsky's rejection. Stiva says Kitty had only a "superficial attraction" for the young officer, that Vronsky's being "such a perfect aristocrat" impressed her mother but not Kitty. Levin's anger at Ryabinin, the fraudulent sale of the forest, and at Vronsky focusses on the concept of "aristocrat". Those like Vronsky or like Ryabinin who gain success by currying favor are not aristocrats, he says. Russia's aristocracy consists of people produced through generations of landowners, not those parasites who deplete and devalue her land and resources for their own gain (like Ryabinin). "I prize what's come to me from my ancestors or been won by hard work," pursues Levin, rather than maintaining myself "by favor of the powerful of this world." He and Stiva part as friends despite the painful subject which could have caused a rift.

Commentary

In these episodes we gain insight into Levin's way of life as a landed proprietor. His dislike of Ryabinin, a land speculator, and his anger at Stiva's cheap sale of the forest derives from a threat to his basic values. This devaluation of valuable property, by a destructive agent who deals in money rather than in values, is a devaluation of resources, tradition, rootedness. Stiva, by his desire for momentary gain, becomes an unwitting tool for undermining the source of Russia's strength and, indeed, the whole existence of "aristocracy", defined by Levin as those who have a vested interest in protecting the basic values of national life. If the peasants cheat landowners out of their property, then at least the land goes to those who deserve it because it is their mainspring of existence. Ryabinin, on the other hand, represents the irresponsible overthrow of the old order; appreciating no values but those of cash and material gain, he intrudes chaos and impoverishment where constructive change and enrichment is required. Vronsky who, like Ryabinin, is uncommitted to the land and basic traditions, whose career is socially and politically oriented, contributes no values to stabilize either himself or other human beings. Kitty's illness, her "devaluation" by Vronsky, proves Levin's point.

Through Levin's arguments, Tolstoy states a general system which generates his philosophy. Human beings must be committed to deeply-rooted values — a personal need corresponding to love — in order to maintain their humanity. Without a source of inner strength, an individual's life becomes empty of meaning and frivolous, capable of destroying other lives besides perverting his own.

CHAPTERS 18 to 25

Summary

While Vronsky's life runs its normal course with its social and military obligations, his passion absorbs his entire inner life. "Society" has various reactions. The younger men envy him; his brother, who enjoys his own extramarital affairs, disapproves because "those whom it was necessary to please" disapprove. His mother thinking an affair in the highest society is "a finishing touch" for a promising young man, disapproves when she hears Alexey refused an important post in order to remain in Petersburg, and when she learns the affair is based upon a desperate, not graceful and worldly, passion. Meanwhile the women of Anna's circle await the turn of public opinion before falling upon her with the full weight of their scorn.

Besides his regimental and social interests, Vronsky is passionately fond of horses and racing. At this time, he has purchased an English thoroughbred and anticipates winning the officers' steeplechase. On the morning of the race he checks his mare, Frou-Frou, and, satisfied she is in the best possible condition, he drives to Anna's house. He resolves to put an end to their impossible position which demands so much lying and deceit. Anna's thoughtful pose impresses him anew with her beauty and grace, and he gazes enraptured until she feels his presence and turns to greet him. Vronsky perceives something new troubling her, but she is reluctant to answer his inquiry. Finally whispering, "I am with child," Anna brings the matter to a head. Vronsky insists that only divorce will "put an end to the deception in which we now live. Our fate is sealed." For fear of losing Seriozha, Anna refuses to consider divorce, but does not mention this to Vronsky. The sound of her son's voice ends their talk, and Vronsky drives to the race.

With mounting excitement, Vronsky watches as the English groom leads Frou-Frou in. Lean and beautiful, she moves as if on springs. Nearby a groom tends a strong, exquisite stallion, the lop-eared Gladiator who is Frou-Frou's chief competitor. Vronsky approaches the starting gate, following his rival Mahotin, Gladiator's rider. They are among seventeen officers competing in the nine hurdle race which runs a three mile elliptical course.

The white-legged Gladiator takes the lead. Frou-Frou, without any urging, increases her speed and draws up to the other horse on the outside, just as Vronsky would have asked her to. His affection for this responsive mount increases. Leading Mahotin's stallion, Vronsky knows he will win, for Frou-Frou's last reserve of strength is more than a match for the final jump. Increasing her speed, the mare clears the ditch. But at that instant, Vronsky makes a dreadful, unforgivable blunder: he drops back — too soon — in the saddle. The white-legged stallion flashes by, while Vronsky, with one foot on the ground feels the mare sink beneath him. Not realizing his clumsy movement has broken her back, he tugs at the reins. Fluttering, she is unable to rise. In a sudden passion, he wrenches the lines, then savagely kicks her belly. A doctor and some officers run up, quickly deciding to shoot the mare. Vronsky leaves the race course; for the first time in his life he knows the bitterest kind of misfortune — misfortune beyond remedy, caused by his own fault.

Commentary

It is significant that Anna's announcement of her pregnancy occurs at the same time Vronsky's passion for horses bears fruit, his imminent victory at the steeplechase. Both situations demand all the resources of which Vronsky is capable in order to meet the challenge. Both crises are confrontations with destiny.

With obvious significance, Dostoevsky remarks that Anna and Vronsky appear to him as a fine mare and full-blooded stallion (an analogy which other critics have also pointed out). Mahotin's stallion wins the race, but the sensitive mare loses her life. The close relationship between rider and mount is akin to Vronsky's bond with Anna. The intensity of their unlawful love is like the intensity of the steeplechase with their life running a course of obstacles which both, as one, must overcome until their race against moral law is won.

But Frou-Frou's entire being exists for racing, Anna's for loving; that the mare breaks her back in fulfilling the purpose of her existence prefigures Anna's subsequent doom. Vronsky, however, does not share his horse's commitment to the race. Though he loves Frou-Frou while they are in the run, his passion for racing is basically frivolous and self-indulgent. The analogy applies to his love affair, where Vronsky, though deeply in love, is not committed to Anna as she is committed to him. That Vronsky's lack of commitment can make him destructive when his mount flounders (he kicks the mare) presages his hostility to Anna when their relationship becomes irritating.

Although Vronsky's horsemanship is unexcelled, Frou-Frou required a perfect rider. And Vronsky had missed perfection by a fatal blunder at the most critical moment. Anna as a sensitive, responsive woman, demanding all-consuming love from her lover, finds Vronsky unequal to meet her exacting requirements. This fatal, irreparable flaw in their relationship drives her to destruction.

The tragedy of the steeplechase, as well as of the doomed liaison, is not a function of Vronsky's horsemanship nor of an inability to love. It is rather a moral tragedy, implicit in human life, occurring whenever an individual confronts crisis. The critical moment provides an "historical necessity" whereby man's imperfectibility defines his destiny.

CHAPTERS 26 to 29

Summary

Despite their changed relationship, Karenin maintains appearances, visiting Anna each week at their summer villa. When they talk, she chats lightly and rapidly, while Karenin, no longer observing the deceit in her entire attitude, responds only to the literal meaning of her words. His hostility, however, expresses itself by an especial coldness to his son. More shy than ever before in front of his father, Seriozha is reduced to silence as Karenin addresses him with an ironical "young man" whenever he speaks to him.

At the race, Karenin watches his wife gaze after one rider, her eyes never observing how horse after horse falls while many officers receive injuries. After Vronsky's fall, Anna weeps with relief to learn he was not killed and accepts Karenin's arm as he leads her from the pavilion. Driving home, Alexey Alexandrovitch remarks on her "unbecoming behavior" in public, repeating his request that she conduct herself to preserve appearance. "I was and I could not help being in despair," replies Anna. "I hear you, but I am thinking of him. I love him, I am his mistress."

His face assumes the solid immobility of the dead. When they arrive home, he informs her in a shaken voice that she must conform to outward propriety until he decides the measures "to secure my honor." Relieved at having spoken, Anna looks forward to meet Vronsky that evening.

Commentary

In these chapters Tolstoy shows how Karenin runs his own "race". by plunging himself deeper into his official work he attempts to escape his thoughts about Anna. However he cannot avoid the obvious truth as he observes Anna at the steeplechase. Karenin finds himself not only at the sidelines of the race course but at the sidelines of a situation which engrosses Anna and Vronsky.

Anna's confession, besides relieving herself of an unstated lie, aims at destroying her husband since she only declares what Karenin already knows but fears. Having told Vronsky, "He (Karenin) doesn't exist," Anna's words seem to carry out her wish, for her husband's face assumed the "solid immobility of the dead." Symbolically ridding herself of him, Anna joyfully anticipates her meeting with Vronsky.

CHAPTERS 30 to 35

Summary
At the German spa, Kitty is strongly attracted by a Russian girl who arrived with an invalid lady named Madame Stahl. She observes how this Mademoiselle Varenka, an adoptive daughter to her companion, makes friends with all who are seriously ill. Varenka's dignity and her absorption in her work—that of performing charitable services for the patients around her—inspire Kitty to emulate her. Despite her pretty face and nice figure, Varenka lacks sensuousness: this is one source of her appeal to Kitty.

Soon after the Shtcherbatskys arrive, two newcomers who provoke "universal and unfavorable attention" appear regularly at the springs. They are a bony Russian man and a pock marked, peasant faced woman named Marya Nicolaevna. When Kitty learns this is Levin's brother Nicolai, she feels disagreeably inclined toward the couple.

Becoming friends with Varenka, Kitty begins to plan her life according to the example of Madame Stahl and her companion. Helping those in trouble, distributing and reading the Gospel to "the sick, and criminal, and the dying" is a career of peace, happiness and goodness for Kitty. Through Varenka, Kitty realizes that to live an exalted life, one must only forget oneself and love others.

Her life's plan backfires humiliatingly. The wife, in one of the families she assists, blames the husband for being infatuated with the young Princess Shtcherbatsky; the woman acts cool, almost rude, to Kitty. Through her father's ironic, critical attitude toward the Pietists (as he calls Madame Stahl and her followers) Kitty realizes the potential hypocrisy of this religious enthusiasm. Her confusion causes her to be disagreeable to Varenka, and after she begs forgiveness of her friend, she gives up this new life's calling. But Kitty does not give up everything she learned from this experience. She becomes aware of her self-deception in "supposing she could be what she wanted to be." She also becomes aware of "all the dreariness in the world of sorrow, of sick and dying people" among whom she lived, and suddenly feeling this oppressive atmosphere, she longs for the fresh air of Russia, of Yerhushovo where Dolly and her family are spending the summer. Kitty returns home cured, no longer carefree and light-hearted, but at peace. The misery she experienced in Moscow is only a memory.

Commentary

Kitty's sojourn at the German spa is the story of her maturation. This period of reflection and purification allows her to accept fulfillment through marriage and family life. Because she violently rejected her womanhood at first, Varenka was Kitty's ideal of perfection. Tolstoy describes Varenka as lacking precisely what Kitty had too much of — "a suppressed fire of vitality and a consciousness of her own attractiveness" — qualities of sensuousness, in other words. As Kitty attempts to live a "soulful" life as Varenka does, she learns it was impossible to deny one's own nature. This became apparent to her when she is accused of turning the head of a married man, although the reader learned this sooner when Kitty immediately rejected the very ill Nicolai Levin. Varenka, Kitty's opposite, learns the same lesson in a different way: later in the novel she is unable to achieve the love of Koznyshev. Both girls submit to their peculiar destiny, Varenka by remaining single and living selflessly, and Kitty by accepting her womanly nature.

PART 3

CHAPTERS 1 to 6

Summary

Koznyshev, deciding to take a vacation, goes to visit his brother, Konstantin Levin. Nothing is more relaxing for Koznyshev than this rural atmosphere; whereas Levin, engulfed in the full tide of summer work, is annoyed at his brother's attitude. Farms and peasants and livestock are part of Levin's life work, while Koznyshev regards this sphere of being merely a refreshment from heavy intellectual labors.

At mowing time, Levin is strongly tempted to join the mowers, but he fears his brother would laugh at him. Finally overpowered by his desire for work and exercise — refreshment from the tiresome intellectual brilliance of Koznyshev, Levin, as casually as possible, orders his scythe sharpened. Working between two peasants, Levin finds it difficult to equal the efforts of the mowers with their untiring muscles. Swinging the scythe with his arm and entire body, Levin concentrates so intensely that all concept of time vanishes. At the noontime break he stays with the peasants, sharing a meal of salted bread with an old man and drinking of the warm river water. Exhausted and exultant, Levin feels at peace.

Koznyshev notes his brother's restored spirits when Levin returns. As they talk together, Levin suspects that Koznyshev's interest in politics, in progressive trends, in the education of the peasants (whom he likes as a class, not as individuals whose experience differs from his own) are only subjects for intellectual exercise. He feels his brother lacks emotional force in all his beliefs.

Koznyshev sums up: "Our differences amount to this," he says, "that you make the mainspring self-interest while I suppose that interest in the common weal exists in every man of a certain degree of advancement." Agreeing with Levin's point that "action founded on material interests would be more desirable," Koznyshev understands that Konstantin, with his own intense, almost primitive, nature requires "intense energetic action or nothing." Appreciating one another's differences, the brothers part affectionately when Koznyshev leaves.

Commentary

Besides defining the differences between the brothers, their arguments represent Levin's own struggle for meaning as he strives to discover the "key to life" first through science, then philosophy, finally concluding that the answer lies in living a "natural life," that is, seeking a universal identity of his soul and that of nature. Koznyshev's emptiness and sterility derive from his dependence on intellectual processes, while Levin's "salvation" derives from his emotional commitment. The exultant feeling of health and peace Levin achieves from mowing prefigures his anti-intellectual solution to life's ultimate meaning.

Levin's "materialism" is based on his confidence in the importance of individual needs. Education, for instance, means nothing to him unless it furthers one's emotional development and deals with increasing one's awareness of basic life goals. For him, peasants do not require education since they understand the basic relation between an individual and his purpose in life. To Koznyshev, education is important for its own sake and must be universally applied so that everyone has intellectual tools with which to understand the complicated problems of an advanced society.

CHAPTERS 7 to 11

Summary

While Oblonsky goes to Petersburg on business, Dolly and her six children move to the country estate at Yergushovo which was part of her dowry. By moving out of Moscow, she avoids the pressing bills of the tradesman which lack of funds prevent her from paying, and her children completely recuperate from their various winter illnesses. Now that her husband no longer loves her, Dolly finds her greatest life pleasure through her children. Meeting Dolly and the youngsters returning from church one morning, Levin exclaims she appeared as "a hen with her chicks" and admires this group of an ideal family. Hearing that Kitty will spend the summer with her sister, he blushes and falls silent. Later he tells Dolly he will not call on her, since Kitty's refusal was final, and any mention of the matter is only a source of pain.

One day in July, Levin drives to the village on his sister's estate to supervise the division of the hay harvest. When it is satisfactorily apportioned, he sits on a haycock to observe the meadow teeming with brightly clad peasants. A young peasant lad loading hay with his pretty bride catches his attention. As the young couple laugh together, he is struck by the strong, young, freshly awakened love which shows in their faces.

Engulfed in this sea of cheerful toil the idea enters his mind that he could, if he wanted to, renounce his artificial, selfish existence with its utterly useless education for this busy, honorable life of simple toil. Deep in thought, Levin leaves the meadow while a chilling night breeze springs up. As a four-in-hand drives by, he sees the serene, thoughtful expression of a girl's face in the window, and then Kitty's candid eyes fall on him. Her face lights up with wonder and surprise, but she does not look out again. As the carriage passes and daylight brightens the sky, Levin makes his decision. "No," he says, "However good that simple life of toil may be, I cannot go back to it, I love *her*."

Commentary

Just as Kitty discovered she could not be untrue to her inner nature, Levin realizes he must follow his destiny. Despite the temptations of the agreeable, natural life of his peasants, he resignedly concludes that he must first find truth and meaning within the bounds of his given nature. As Kitty passes by on her way to Dolly's estate, Levin recognizes his commitment to the life he now leads. Before he can change his career, he must first wrestle with his present way of life and discover its basic values. Thus, on an individual level, Tolstoy shows how Levin struggles for meaning within the bounds of his own "historical necessity."

CHAPTERS 12 TO 23

Summary

At Anna's confession, Karenin remins still and deathlike. After seeing her home, he is better able to examine the problem. Like a sufferer
who has had the bad tooth extracted, he feels relief at his wife's outburst.
Despite his deep cowardice, he first considers challenging Vronsky to a
duel. Karenin decides that, being indispensable to the ministry, he should
allow nothing to interfere either with his duties or his reputation; no, a
duel would solve nothing. Legal divorce, or even separation, is also not
feasible, since the resulting scandal would injure only himself and the guilty
parties would be united; they should rather suffer from their crimes. His
only recourse is to keep his wife with him, conceal from the world what had
happened, use every measure in his power to break off the intrigue, and
above all (though he does not admit this) to punish her. His decision
pleases him, and he feels satisfied that religious sanction coincides so con-
veniently with his self-interest. He resolves to write Anna a letter announcing his decision to maintain the status quo.

When he arrives home in Petersburg, Karenin first writes to Anna,
then turns to an official matter, the business of setting up a commission
to inquire into the work of the Native Tribes Organization Committee.
Having accomplished both important items of work, Karenin retires,
well pleased with himself.

Despite contradicting Vronsky when he said their position was an
impossible one, Anna too desires above all to put an end to her false and
dishonorable marriage. But where would she turn if put out of her husband's house? In her distress she imagines that Vronsky, loving her less,
already finds her a burden. No, she cannot offer herself to him. Besides
miserable, Anna is frightened: in her new spiritual condition she feels
everything in her soul is double, each part claimed by conflicting loyalties
to the two men in her life. If her relations to Vronsky and Karenin are in
question, there is no ambivalence about Seriozha. Her aim and only support in life is her son. But she must act quickly to secure his helpless position. Ordering her things packed, she decides to leave with him for Moscow.

Then she reads Karenin's note which just arrived, and feels her plight
more awful than ever. Shuddering at his threat that he would take her son
if she persists in her unlawful ways, Anna finds her husband's insistence
to lead the same life they always live further evidence of his willingness to
exist by lies and hypocrisy. Enraged and frustrated, she realizes she is not
strong enough to escape this intolerable situation. Never able to know

freedom in love, she would remain the guilty wife constantly threatened with exposure, deceiving her husband for a disgraceful liaison with a man whose life she could not share. Weeping unconstrainedly, Anna cannot conceive how it will end. Later that afternoon she attends Princess Betsy's croquet party, leaving early to meet Vronsky at six o'clock.

As he does four or five times a year, Vronsky spends that day figuring his accounts and putting all his affairs in order. Despite his frivolous life, he hates irregularity and always manages his finances with care. He calls this day of reckoning a *faire de lessive,* and at this point, Tolstoy also reckons up the course of Vronsky's life.

Throughout his career, Vronsky has lived by a code of principles which answers problems in his life: "gambling debts must be paid, the tailor need not be; one must not lie to a man but might to a woman; one must never cheat anyone but may a husband; one must not pardon insults, but one may insult others, and so on." Lately, however, Vronsky finds these rules do not withstand the present contingencies of his intense love. Now that Anna's pregnancy means their lives must be joined, he wonders if he is prepared to make the necessary sacrifices. Ambition in his career rivals his passion for Anna, and he envies his good friend and school comrad, Serpuhovskoy who had become a general and now expects a command with great political influence. When they meet at a party, Serpuhovskoy tactfully tells Vronsky that women are the chief obstacles to a man's career. Marriage clears the path, however, and he begs Vronsky to give him *carte blanche* permission to use his influence in advancing his friend. Russia needs men like you in her service, he tells the officer. Promising to think it over, Vronsky goes to meet Anna.

When he reads Karenin's note to Anna, and she tells of her confession, he joyfully thinks "a duel is now inevitable" and pictures that honorable moment when, after firing into the air, he awaits the shot of the outraged husband. Serpuhovskoy's advice flashes through his mind — that it is better not to bind oneself — and he knows he cannot mention this thought to Anna. Seeing the lack of determination in his face, Anna loses hope.

"Things cannot remain as he supposes," says Vronsky, thinking of the duel but saying something else. She must leave her husband. "But my son!" cries Anna, "I should have to leave him and I can't and won't do that." To Vronsky the choice is simple: she must leave her child or maintain this degrading position. "To whom is it degrading?" says Anna. The only thing important in her life is Vronsky's love, and "if that's mine, I feel so exalted...that nothing can humiliate me." As she sobs, Vronsky, himself close to tears, feels helpless knowing he is to blame for her wretchedness. Sadly, Anna realizes her fears: everything will remain the same.

That Monday, at the usual sitting of the Commission, Karenin emerges victorious. His motion carried after a fight, even against the arguments of his rival Stremov, three new commissions are appointed to investigate the Reorganization of the Native Tribes. Petersburg society talks of nothing else but Karenin's latest victory.

The next day Anna arrives in Petersburg, her visit marring Karenin's satisfaction from yesterday's triumph. Demanding his wife's conduct to be above the suspicions of even the servants, Karenin forbids Anna to meet her lover. In return, he allows her all the privileges of a respectable wife without fulfilling the duties of one.

Commentary

These chapters define the characters of Karenin and Vronsky, and with Anna Arkadyevna caught "double-souled" between them, they have reached a stalemate. Both men have gone as far as their characters and experiences allow them to go. Until a crisis, the situation is to remain static.

Vronsky is a representative character of the milieu of army and court nobility which has made his career. His motivations are socially conditioned according to his social role and function as a promising career man in the military. Guided by his "code of behavior" Vronsky concludes a duel will occur, thus solving the problem of his honor. With confusion, he realizes that a duel will not solve Anna's disgrace. Now that her condition demands his assuming responsibility for her future, a resolve he has not yet decided, Vronsky's imagination stops.

Karenin, shown as almost the very symbol of bureaucracy, approaches his domestic problems the same way he meets problems at the office. Tolstoy tells us this as Alexey Alexandrovitch first dispatches a letter to Anna, then turns to the business of the Native Tribes Commission. Karenin sees Vronsky as an enemy like Stremov, a rival to be overcome through political, rather than personal, application. Human impulses are sunk deep within him. Religion, whose principles he applies as an afterthought, is for Karenin just a set of highly institutionalized rules. Since a duel solves no problems for a bureaucrat, Karenin issues no challenge. He must compromise emotional problems and avoid their poignancy through the principle of expediency.

38

CHAPTERS 24 to 32

The after effects of Levin's evening on the haycock destroy his pleasure as a squire and make him dissatisfied with farming. He is additionally annoyed because Kitty is spending the summer merely twenty miles away. Seeking a change, Levin visits his friend Sviazhsky who lives in a remote part of the district with splendid snipe marshes nearby.

Although the hunting is poor, Levin's discussions with Sviazhsky and another guest about the state of the Russian peasant and the inefficient use of the land inspire him to devise a new system of agriculture. After a few days, he hastens home to put his plan into action. Levin wants to increase the peasants' interest in the success of their work, even if it means, temporarily, that new methods and new machinery be sacrificed. He plans that he and the peasants work as shareholders in the estate. One stumbling-block is that summer farming is in full swing. Another is the insurmountable distrust of the peasants; they cannot believe that the master has any other aim than to squeeze all he can out of them. Some of the peasants grasp the idea of cooperative land plots and parts of the farm are divided accordingly, the rest of the estate remaining as before. Problems arise, of course, and some of the peasants do not put in the improvements they had agreed upon. These matters, along with managing the rest of the estate and writing a book on the subject occupy Levin until well in September.

Late one evening a visitor arrives. Hearing the familiar sound of coughing, Levin runs downstairs to greet his brother Nicolai. He has come, as Levin requested, to receive his share of a recently sold family estate. Although happy to see him, Levin feels frightened as he kisses the dry skin and looks into the unnaturally glittering eyes. Death, since it marks his own brother, confronts him for the first time and with an expecially irresistible force.

Despite their deep affection, their conversation is insincere and disagreeable. Though Levin knows his brother is trying to hide his fear of death, he is stung by the bitter criticisms the sick man makes of his new system. Nicolai accuses him of being communistic, that Levin lacking conviction just reorganizes the peasants to flatter his self-esteem. After Nicolai leaves, Levin sees death or the advances of death in everything. He works harder than ever to realize his scheme, feeling this the one thread to guide him through the ever impending darkness.

Commentary

Levin's farming scheme is an "action founded on material interests," to quote Koznyshev, aimed at the efficient use of available resources of land and labor so that the peasants, as well as the master, gain profit. Unnecessary waste is repulsive to Levin (exemplified at his disgust over Stiva's careless sale of the valuable forest) who believes that long-term reforms and basic life goals are based on materialist considerations. Levin's passion for agronomic reform satisfies his need for arduous work and expresses his search for meaning through emotional commitment rather than through intellectual inquiry. Criticizing his brother's reforms for showing his lack of conviction, Nicolai echoes Levin's deep-seated anxieties. Konstantin suspects himself of the same fault, fearing his zeal for reform merely as an avoidance of a deeper issue. Nicolai is right; Levin attempts to avoid the "deeper issue" of death, and with his brother's condition forcing him to confront the problem, Konstantin begins to struggle with this grave threat.

Levin's materialism derives from his attachment to sensual reality. His intense nature drives him to search for the meaning of his life through the everyday actions of his human individuality. Levin's desire for marriage and family is also based on this search. Love and his future offspring are essential to his self-fulfillment as a human being. As a further tie to his immediate world, marriage increases his sense of reality. But death has no part of Levin's life-seeking scheme and his attempt to come to terms with this threat becomes an obsessive struggle that carries him through the rest of the novel.

PART 4

CHAPTERS 1 to 23

Summary

Although totally estranged, the Karenins live as before. Anna continues to meet Vronsky but always away from home and her husband knows about it. All three endure their misery only because they hope for a change. Karenin expects this passion to pass with the lapse of time, while Anna hopes "something" will turn up to settle the situation. Vronsky, submitting to her lead, waits for the problem to clear up of itself without his taking any action.

In the middle of winter, Vronsky spends a tiresome week showing a foreign prince the sights of the city. A "true gentleman," the visitor is a stupid, self-satisfied, immaculate person. Dignified and poised with his superiors, free and simple with his equals, contemptuously indulgent with his inferiors, the visitor is a disturbing mirror-image of Vronsky himself. When the foreigner finally leaves, Vronsky so relieved to be delivered from this distasteful self-reflection, engages in an all night revel to purge himself.

Returning home, Vronsky finds a note from Anna asking him to see her while Karenin is at a meeting. At her gate, Vronsky alights from his sledge only to come face to face with Alexey Alexandrovitch just entering his carriage. As they bow coldly to one another, Vronsky feels like a snake in the grass, a position foreign to his nature which angers and frustrates him.

Having heard about his latest revel, Anna feels more wretched than ever and scolds him in one of her more and more frequent fits of jealousy. Though he knows she is prompted out of her great love for him, Vronsky takes fright at her outburst. At these moments his love vanishes, and he notes her increasing stoutness, her somewhat faded beauty and the new spiteful expression which sometimes crosses her face. Yet he feels the bond between them can never be broken. Asking her what the doctor had said, Vronsky learns their child shall arrive soon. Their position will then be resolved, says Anna, but not as they expect. Tears well in her eyes and she feels sorry for him. "Soon·we shall be at peace and suffer no more," she says. "And I shall not live through it."

Karenin storms directly to Anna's rooms when he returns. Furious that she dared see Vronsky at their home, he declares he will see a lawyer and begin divorce proceedings. Seriozha is to remain with his sister until the case is decided. "Leave me Seriozha," Anna pleads, "You don't love him. You want him in order to hurt me." "Yes," answers Karenin in his fury, "I associate my son with my loathing for you." Anna begs that Seriozha remain until after her confinement; at that Karenin loses his temper completely and flings from the room. The next day he engages a famous Petersburg lawyer to take the case.

Karenin's previous victory at the last sitting of the commission turns into defeat. With full information about the condition of the native tribes (gathered through all the administrating officials in these remote parts) his enemy, Stremov, goes over to his side, carrying other members with him. Not only agreeing with Karenin, Stremov proposes even more radical solutions to the problem so that, carried to an extreme, the measures prove ridiculous. The commission divides in confusion, no one knowing whether the native tribes are flourishing or impoverished. All the indignation of public opinion and of officialdom falls on Karenin. Owing to the contempt of those who know Karenin's domestic life, as well as this last blunder, his position is somewhat precarious. To remedy matters, Karenin resolves to travel — at his own expense — to the distant provinces and investigate for himself the condition of the native tribes.

Stopping in Moscow for three days, Karenin meets Oblonsky. To get rid of his brother-in-law, Alexey Alexandrovitch agrees to dine at the Oblonskys the following evening. Stiva is delighted to have Karenin as the most distinguished guest for his party where Kitty and Levin are also to attend. This occasion emphasizes his recently happy life. Although still short of money, he manages to provide fine gifts for the pretty actress he has recently taken under his protection, and Dolly has been quite cheerful for a time.

Returning from church, Karenin sets to work. He writes to the lawyer, enclosing some of Vronsky's letters to Anna as evidence, and then receives a deputation for the native tribes on the way to Petersburg. Then the servant announces Oblonsky. Stiva begs Alexey Alexandrovitch to reconsider the divorce. At least Karenin must talk to Dolly before going any further with proceedings.

One of the last to arrive at his home, Oblonsky perceives at first glance that his guests are not yet brought together. In a moment he has introduced everyone to everyone else. Bringing Koznyshev and Karenin together on a talk about the russification of Poland, Stiva has the conversation lively and his company relax and begin enjoying themselves.

At Levin'a arrival, Kitty's face lights up with joy and she almost bursts into tears. To Levin her every word holds unutterable meaning and his whole being is filled with tenderness for her. While everyone else discusses women's right, Levin and Kitty talk softly together, delighted at their perfect understanding.

Meantime Dolly draws Karenin off for a talk. She begins by protesting Anna's innocence, but Karenin's response cuts her short. She tries to change his mind — "anything but a divorce," she pleads — appealing to his sense of Christian charity. But even after the intense discussion, Karenin's opinion remains the same.

Levin and Kitty talk at a card table while she scribbles with a chalk. He is amazed that their minds are in such perfect agreement. However badly he expresses a thought, she always understands. Taking the chalk from her, he writes only the initial letters of his question: "When you told me it could not be—did that mean never or then?" Pointing to the "n," Kitty says, "That means 'never' but it's not true." A few more sentences pass between them with the chalk, and then Levin writes the initials for, "I have never ceased to love you." With this device he asks her to marry him and Kitty answers "Yes" before he finishes writing. When the Shtcherbatskys leave, Levin feels so forlorn without her that he can hardly await the next morning to call on them.

After the dinner, Levin accompanies his brother Koznyshev to a meeting. Filled with joy, he finds everyone splendid and good-hearted. Levin listens to the debate on missing sums of money and the laying of sewer pipes. He concludes that the subject is unimportant to the debating members and that they merely enjoy themselves.

Levin's excitement allows him no rest that night. Toward noon the next day he arrives at the Shtcherbatskys and Kitty runs to meet him. The old prince and princess are kind and affectionate; both have tears in their eyes. Then the servants offer congratulations, and then relations begin to arrive. This is the beginning of the "blissful hubbub" which never diminishes until the wedding.

Levin feels Kitty has much to forgive. One matter is his lack of faith, but his betrothed does not care. She says she knows his soul and in it sees the goodness she values. The other item concerns his past life, and Levin regrets he is not as chaste as she. Wishing to share all his secrets, he gives her his diary, and Kitty weeps bitterly over the notebook. This confession is the one painful episode of their engagement. When she forgives him, Levin feels more than ever unworthy of her love. Morally bowed before her, he prizes his great undeserved happiness more highly than before.

Returning to his lodgings, Karenin recalls his talk with Dolly. Annoyed at her reminder of Christian forgiveness—"love those that hate you"—Karenin turns to consider his tour of inspection in the provinces. First he reads his two telegrams. One contains news that Stemov received the very appointment he had coveted for himself. The second is from Anna. "I am dying," she writes. "I beg, I implore you to come. I shall die easier with your forgiveness." Realizing her confinement is near, he decides the note is not just a trick. He will leave for Petersburg right away, perform his last duty to her, retaining his self respect despite everything. But he cannot drive away the reflection that her death would solve his most pressing problem.

At home Karenin learns she had been safely delivered yesterday but she is very ill now. Entering Anna's room he finds Vronsky, face in hands, weeping at her writing table. Karenin's appearance confuses him. "She is dying," Vronsky says, "The doctors say there is no hope. I am entirely in your hands, only let me remain here." Turning from his tears, Karenin approaches Anna's bed. With flushed cheeks, glittering eyes, she talks rapidly in a ringing voice. She speaks of Seriozha, and of her husband who does not himself know how good he is. Karenin's face quivers as he sees her gaze at him with such tender and ecstatic affection as he has never seen in her before.

"Don't be surprised at me," Anna says. "There is another woman in me (who) loved that man and tried to hate you...Now I'm my real self, all myself. I'm dying now. Only one thing I want: forgive me, forgive me completely..."

Suddenly Karenin gives way to an emotion which gives him a new happiness he has never known. Kneeling, with his head against her arm which burns like fire through his sleeve, he sobs. She calls Vronsky, who, seeing Anna, buries his face in his hands. "Uncover your face!" she orders. "Look at him! He is a saint!" To her husband she cries, "Uncover his face, Alexey Alexandrovitch, I want to see him!" Karenin draws Vronsky's hands away, uncovering a look terrible in its agony and shame. "Give him your hand," says Anna, "Forgive him." Karenin stretches out his hand," while unrestrained tears stream down his cheeks. "Thank God, thank God," murmurs Anna. Then the pains begin again. Crying for morphia, she tosses about on the bed.

Anna had puerperal fever, the doctors said, and ninety-nine cases out of a hundred are fatal. In a coma, Anna's end is moments away. Toward morning she regains consciousness, then sleeps again. The doctors are hopeful.

That day, Karenin comes to Vronsky in the boudoir. The luminous, serene expression of his tear filled eyes impresses Vronsky. "The happiness of forgiving has revealed to me my duty," the husband tells him. "Should the world hold me a laughing-stock, I will never forsake her and will never utter a word of reproach to you." Promising to call should Anna wish to see him, Karenin suggests that Vronsky leave.

As if in a stupor, Vronsky stands on the steps. All the rules of his familiar world now seem false and inapplicable. Anna had raised her deceived husband to an elevated position from which that despised creature proves himself, not ludicrous or false, but kind, straightforward, and dignified. Their positions are reversed: Karenin exalted, magnaminous, himself debased, petty, and deceitful. Feeling further dejected since his love for Anna had increased during her illness, Vronsky has been humiliated before her at the very pinnacle of his love and has now lost her forever. Returning to his brother's house, Vronsky finds rest impossible even after his vigil of three days and nights. Out of desperation and wretchedness he aims his gun at his heart and fires. With consciousness dropping from him, Vronsky is suddenly aware that he has missed.

In the following weeks, Karenin basks in his feeling of inward peace. Now that he freely loves and freely forgives, he finds life so simple. He has a great affection for the newborn daughter and visits the nursery many times a day. Yet he feels the world will not understand him, that something more is expected of him. Though realizing his relations with Anna are still unstable and unnatural, Karenin does not want the situation to change.

The "misunderstanding world" for Karenin is best represented by the stylish Betsy Tverskoy who has just arrived with a message for Anna. Vronsky had written to beg Anna to see him once more before he departs to a new post at Tashkent, a distant province. A little afraid of her husband, Anna asks his advice, but Karenin cannot express himself under Betsy's contemptuous gaze. He is relieved when Betsy leaves them. Karenin is aware of Anna's irritation in his presence. His physical proximity repulses her. Deciding never to see Vronsky again, Anna feels the misery of her false position with full strength. "Oh God, why didn't I die," she sobs.

Realizing Anna's hatred of him, and realizing that the world demands their divorce, Karenin is in a dilemma. Divorce would place Anna in a helpless position, disgrace both children, and deprive himself of everything he cares for. Yet he realizes that the world would prevail against what he thinks is right and proper.

Oblonsky arrives while the Princess Betsy is leaving. Finding his sister in misery, Stiva tries to convince Karenin to consent to divorce. After they discuss the matter, Alexey Alexandrovitch gives Stiva permission to arrange matters as he sees fit.

Vronsky hovers between life and death in the days following his attempted suicide. His action solved one source of his misery and he can confront Karenin's magnaminity without humiliation. Resolving that he would no longer come between the repentant wife and her husband, he accepts a post which Serpuhovskoy found for him and asks Betsy to arrange a final meeting with Anna before he leaves for Tashkent.

Betsy arrives with news that Karenin has consented to a divorce. Vronsky dashes to Anna's house. Without looking to see whether they are alone or not, he showers kisses on her, while Anna trembles with emotion. Finally able to speak, Anna tells him she wants no divorce, that she is worried about Seriozah. Tears flow down her cheeks, and she is unable to smile.

Vronsky refuses his Tashkent post, and, noting the disapproval from high quarters at this action, quickly resigns his commission. A month later Karenin and his son are left alone in the house. Anna goes abroad with Vronsky, not having obtained a divorce and having resolutely refused one.

Commentary

This section presents the parallel careers of Levin and Anna in striking contrast. As Levin embarks to fulfill his life through his courtship and marriage to Kitty, we see his career as an affirmation of his life. This part of his story already points to the happy ending in his struggle to overcome death. Anna's imminent death in this section, however, portends disaster.

Just as death reverses life, Anna's deathbed crisis reverses the process of her love affair. From this point on, we see the slow-motion deterioration of her relationship with Vronsky and its corresponding effect on her lover and husband.

As Vronsky and Karenin exchange roles during this crisis, they both achieve an emotional intensity neither have previously experienced. At the point of losing Anna, Vronsky rises to the pinnacle of his love but finds himself unable to cope with his humiliation and debasement. With Karenin exalted, Vronsky's "code of prescribed behavior" offers no solution to his present crisis. His life based on regimented social values to sustain his ego, Vronsky cannot countenance this sudden loss of honor. He responds by trying to destroy his suddenly meaningless life now that it can no longer conform to formulistic interpretation. Tolstoy shows us that Vronsky is too rigid to sustain the intensity of his passion. The attempted suicide tells us of the ultimate futility of Vronsky's attempt to maintain the emotional depth of love that Anna demands from him.

For Karenin, Anna's deathbed crisis acts as a catalyst releasing his latent emotions of love and forgiveness—emotions which he has spent his life trying to repress. His exaltation results from his sudden discovery of universal love and the truth of "turning the other cheek," a basic tenet in Tolstoyan Christianity. No longer resisting evil, Karenin's confrontation with evil allows him to overcome it. Death for Alexey Alexandrovitch becomes the basic truth which makes him a living human being capable of love.

With a masterful touch of irony, Tolstoy also brings Anna to a point of reversal when she is near death. In her fever, Anna's "real self" begs forgiveness while she gazes with tender affection at her husband. However, when she returns to health, Anna chooses in favor of Vronsky. Tolstoy's device here is a Dostoevskian twist to show how the moment of death illuminates life's truths, whereas the state of health provides the conditions for illusion.

This awareness of life-in-death provides the climax of the novel, with the main characters perceiving truth from the heights of their emotional intensity. Hate and deceit no longer exist in the presence of death, and Anna, Vronsky, and Karenin live a moment of pure innocence. From the point of Anna's recovery, however, the novel portrays the human condition as if after the Fall of Grace. Karenin, despite his ennoblement, finds Anna cannot love him. Vronsky pursues his ill-fated love, while Anna follows through toward her already doomed destiny.

Thus Tolstoy provides a crossroad in this section of the novel, defining the direction his main characters will take from now on. Levin's path ascends toward light and love, while Anna's career points to tragedy.

PART 5

CHAPTERS 1 to 6

Summary

Stiva tells Levin he needs a certificate of confession before he can be married. Levin appears in church, confessing to the old priest his sin of doubting everything, even the existence of God. After receiving absolution, he ponders over the priest's questions as to how he will provide for his children's "spiritual advancement in the light of truth."

Levin dines with his bachelor friends the night before the wedding. Koznyshev points out that a wife interferes with her husband's pleasures. But Levin considers his greatest happiness is being with Kitty and following her wishes.

Suddenly unsure of what her wishes are, he is even jealous of Vronsky all over again. Seeking Kitty, Levin asks her if she is sure she wants to marry him. She bursts into tears, and when calm again, explains why she loves him: because she understands him perfectly, because she knows what he would like, and everything he likes is good.

The wedding takes place the next day, and the young couple leave for the country that evening.

Commentary

With communion, the bachelor party, the long church ceremony, Levin undergoes the rites-of-passage into this new phase of his life. He is happy from a feeling of freedom — not the type of egocentric, intellectual liberty Koznyshev defends — but a freedom derived from the emotional satisfactions of his new relationship with Kitty. Levin's last minute doubts, Kitty's mixed feelings as she anticipates her new life, their fumbling during parts of the church ceremony, are minor adjustments which prefigure the major adjustments both Kitty and Levin undergo during their first period of life together.

CHAPTERS 7 to 13

Summary

During the three months that Anna and Vronsky travel abroad, they are sensitive to the reactions of their acquaintances. Avoiding contact with Russians, they discover that most people they know are tactful about their illegal relationship.

In this first period of freedom and rapid return to health, Anna feels "unpardonably happy," and her illness, the crisis of Karenin's attitude, leavetaking from her son, seem like parts of a fevered dream. Vronsky's presence is a continual delight for her. He is constantly attentive, showing no regret for sacrificing a promising career for her sake. Although seeking imperfections in Vronsky, Anna can find none.

Vronsky, however, soon learns that happiness "does not consist merely in the realizing of one's desires." After a period of contentment, he feels ennui. To fill sixteen leisure hours each day, he devotes himself to a succession of intense interests: first politics, then books, now painting. Although finding himself somewhat talented, his study and practice of art is brief. Vronsky realizes how shallow his talent is when they become acquainted with a Russian painter living in the same Italian town.

Abandoning his own portrait of Anna, he commissions the artist to paint her picture. Without this occupation, their life suddenly becomes boring. They decide to return to Russia and settle in the country. Anna plans to visit her son in Petersburg, while Vronsky intends business with his brother and divide their property.

Commentary

Despite the happiness of her honeymoon, Anna is threatened by memories of her past as well as by the insecurity of her future. This insecurity is represented by the careful way in which Anna and Vronsky choose their circle of friends, for Vronsky's nature is dependent upon society for his fulfillment. Although he bravely represses his regrets for the past, Vronsky's feelings are implicit in his restless search for a calling beyond the demands of his love. The basic frivolity of his pursuits underlines once more the basic frivolity of his love. Tolstoy implies that Vronsky and Anna can be happy and at peace if they are away from the pressures of urban society. But the test of their relationship is yet to come when they return to the city and try to settle accounts with the past they have left behind in Petersburg.

CHAPTERS 14 to 20

Summary

Despite their great love, the first period of Levin's married life is a trying one. Not knowing what is important to each of them, they have frequent arguments. After each quarrel, however, they experience a renewed tenderness and reaffirmation of their love. Only during their third month of marriage, after a four week stay in Moscow, does life begin to run smoothly.

Working on his book explaining his system of land reform, with Kitty embroidering near him, Levin recalls how he used to write in order to subdue the feeling of all-pervading death. Now he works to subdue the feeling of "unspeakable brightness" and joy. Having always believed that marriage was the time one started the business of life most seriously, Levin marvels at his months of idleness, for he has not done farm work or touched his book since his wedding. He does not understand Kitty's idleness and lack of "serious" interests derive from her instincts of nest building. Tolstoy explains that Kitty is preparing herself for the time when housekeeping and child raising become the total significance of her life.

Levin receives a letter from Marya Nicolaevna which tells that his brother is dying, and prepares to leave for Moscow. Kitty insists to accompany him, despite Levin's reluctance to have his wife confront a "fallen woman."

They arrive at the dilapidated, dirty country inn where Nicolai Levin and Masha are staying. Levin is repulsed by the dirt and disorder of the sickroom, by the writhing and groaning of the living corpse which is his brother. Kitty sits by Nicolai's bed, holding his hand and comforting him by sympathetic, unoffending words. She orders a better room for Nicolai, supervises the maid at dusting and scrubbing, has fresh linen put on the bed, fresh clothes for the patient, sends for the doctor, the chemist, summons the waiter. Nicolai has a new expression of hope on his face as he is freshly attired, resting comfortably in a sweet smelling orderly room. At Kitty's urging, he agrees to receive the sacrament and extreme unction. But his only faith, he whispers to Levin, rests in the phial of opium which releases him from his constant pain. For three days, Nicolai hovers on the brink of death. The long vigil is a terrible physical and emotional strain on those around him. When his brother finally dies, Levin is in utter despair at the enormity of death. He must cling more strongly than ever to life, to love. At this point, he learns that Kitty is pregnant.

Commentary

Out of more than two hundred chapters, only the one dealing with Nicolai's last illness has a title. This chapter—Chapter 20—called "Death," had great significance for Tolstoy, wherein he records the death of his own brother. The moment holds tremendous significance for Levin as well. He discovers more poignantly than ever that the mysteries of existence are not revealed to the intellect. Only an emotional experience can provide an individual with tools to accept the fact of death. While Levin finds himself still blocked at confronting death, Kitty is able to handle the situation. Marveling at his wife's intuitive ability to confront sickness and death, Levin remarks to himself, "Thou hast hid things from the wise and prudent and hast revealed them unto babes." Until he can renounce intellectual seeking to life's problems, Levin will still lack self-fulfillment. Kitty, on the other hand, fulfills her human destiny because she has no intellectual orientation.

CHAPTERS 21 to 33

Summary

Karenin finds himself alone and despised by all, as a sick dog left by the pack to fend for itself. At the deepest point in his misery, Countess Lydia Ivanovna enters his study unannounced and offers herself as his confidante and helper. Doing what she can to "lighten his burden of petty cares" the countess begins to run Karenin's household. Despite having considered her religiosity excessive and distasteful, Karenin is comforted by her prayers and exhortations. Lydia Ivanovna begins her management by telling Seriozha that his father is a saint and his mother is dead. Then she attends to the practical household affairs, though proving herself inept. Karenin's valet, Korney, quietly corrects her impossible orders, and things run smoothly under his guidance.

Lydia Ivanovna is given to excesses. She frequently falls in love, especially with people connected with the court, and now directs all her affections at Karenin. She is especially proud of having converted Alexey Alexandrovitch from an apathetic believer into a fervent Christian. With her usual blindness, she does not realize his belief is merely a convenient way for him to overcome his humiliation and misery. She is, of course, very jealous of Anna, and gives no answer to Madame Karenina's request to see Seriozha.

Karenin takes great care to provide his son with an excellent education. Hiring outstanding tutors in each discipline, he himself gives Seriozha lessons in the New Testament.

Seriozha, meanwhile, does not believe that his mother is dead. His favorite occupation during his walks is to look for her. Every comely, dark-haired woman sends such a rush of tenderness through him that his eyes fill with tears. He imagines how his mother would come to him, her smiling face revealed as she raises her veil to kiss him.

Arriving at Petersburg, Anna thinks of nothing but her son and how to meet him. Humiliated at the countess' lack of response, Anna's shame turns to wrath when Lydia Ivanovna does write, saying that Seriozha's ideals would be shattered by his mother's presence.

She enters the house early one morning and goes to her son's room. Seriozha has become a young boy since her absence, thinner, taller, more mature. Aching with love, Anna hugs him while he is still asleep. Finding his mother is a reality, not a delicious dream, Seriozha wriggles in her arms and presses closely against her.

Anna returns to her hotel room so dazed she does not know why she is there. Despite her intense longing, and having prepared her emotions for the meeting, she has been unable to foresee how violently the encounter would affect her. Now the nurse brings in the newly dressed baby girl, whose round pink face wreathes in smiles when she sees her mother. Yet Anna feels her love for little Ani is nowhere as intense as that reserved for her son, the first child on whom she lavished all the affection she could not give its father.

Gazing at her son's photograph, she sees a picture of Vronsky on the same page of the album, suddenly remembering he is the cause of her present misery. Along with a surge of love for Vronsky, she reproaches him in her mind for not being here to share her unhappiness. Perhaps he does not love her, she thinks, and finds all sorts of evidence to prove it: their separate hotel suites, the guest Vronsky brings with him rather than seeing her alone.

When Vronsky and Anna meet for dinner that evening, he finds her in an unusual reckless mood. She has invited guests to dine with them, flirts with the men, and, suddenly, decides to attend a benefit performance at the opera that night where all Petersburg will be there to see her. Your presence will acknowledge your position as a fallen woman, Vronsky wants to say to Anna. Begging her not to go, he tries not to look at her beauty, now heightened by the gown she will wear to the theater. Anna cries out that for her nothing matters but her love for Vronsky, that she does not regret what she has done.

Arriving when the performance is in full swing, Vronsky goes to Anna's box at intermission. He learns that she has been insulted by the countess in the next box, and her name is on everyone's lips as people throng the halls. Only at home does Anna succumb to the emotions her humiliation has aroused. She blames him for her shame, and Vronsky can comfort her only by repeated assurances of his love. Her dazzling beauty irritates him, and in his heart he reproaches her action. The next day, fully reconciled, they leave for the country.

Commentary

Anna's heart-rending visit to her son affects her the same way as his brother's death affected Levin: both cling more intensely to their love and life after experiencing a loss. Strengthened in her love according to the amount of suffering she paid for it, Anna defends her rights to happiness against the very society opposed to it. She declares the truth of her status by appearing in public. Quoting Steiner, "the ironic intensity" of the scene derives from its setting: "society condemns Anna precisely in that place where society is most frivolous, ostentatious, and steeped in illusion."

She blames Vronsky for her humiliation because he lacks the depth of soul to understand her torment at giving up Seriozha. Anna feels her challenge would have been a triumph had Vronsky been proud of her public declaration. Instead, like Karenin before him, Vronsky, perplexed at her wilful neglect of propriety, thinks only to hide his disgrace from the members of his social set. The moment of disagreement reveals Vronsky's limitations. At her public and proud affirmation of her love for him, he loses respect for her. He is even regretful of being attracted by her beauty, as if her physical charms were to blame for this embarrassment.

Thus Tolstoy shows the fateful differences between Vronsky and Anna. For Vronsky, love is not an absolute quality, but one which must be reinforced through its environment. Unfavorable circumstances wear love's intensity while Anna's love, under the same conditions, becomes more intense and desperate. This is another example of Tolstoy's concept of "historical necessity" which molds the human condition. Once Anna and Vronsky are isolated from Petersburg society, however, their lives run smoothly and the failing balance of their relationship is restored.

PART 6

CHAPTERS 1 to 5

Summary
Levin's household at Pokrovskoe is filled with summer guests he calls the "Schtcherbatsky element" although Koznyshev is also there. These include Dolly, her children and governesses, the old princess (supervising Kitty's pregnancy), Kitty's father, and Varenka who finally fulfills her promise to visit when Kitty is married.

Koznyshev's interest in Varenka causes everyone to hope for their marriage. Koznyshev was once betrothed to a girl when Levin was a child. When she died, Koznyshev vowed never to fall in love again. On this occasion, however, he decided to ask Varenka in marriage and the moment of declaration arrives when they find themselves alone during a mushroom hunting expedition. Nervous in the pregnant silence, Koznyshev and Varenka talk about the difference between two mushroom varieties. Their tension subsides, and each is somewhat relieved. "I cannot be untrue to the memory of Marie," thinks Koznyshev as they walk quietly and slightly abashed toward the rest of the company.

Commentary
Tolstoy implies that intellectuality leads to a self-centered sterility. Koznyshev's rational approach to life, and Varenka's abstract piety, prevent them from experiencing an intense human relationship. As these passion-denying individuals accept their lonely destiny, Tolstoy compares their empty existence with the flesh and blood love Kitty and Levin experience and which enriches their lives with significance and self-fulfillment. The emphasis here is on the "natural life" where one loves and procreates,

as opposed to the "unnatural life" where one lives by abstract principles. Natural man, says Tolstoy again and again, grasps life through all its realities and can then understand death. Intellect and spirit merely bypass essential truths.

CHAPTERS 6 to 15

Summary

Stepan Arkadyevitch arrives that afternoon with another guest named Vassenka Veslovsky. Good-natured and handsome, brilliant in society, the newcomer has just spent some time at Vronsky's estate fifty miles hence. Although Vassenka makes a favorable impression on everyone else, Levin dislikes him, for he seems to pay especial court to Kitty. When Dolly, the old princess, and Kitty eagerly listen to Vassenka's stories at dinner, Levin's jealousy intensifies. He imagines that Kitty is already in love with Vassenka and perhaps has even planned a rendezvous. Later, Levin blurts out his suspicions to Kitty. She explains that she listened so intensely to Vassenka because he told them of Anna's life with Vronsky. Levin feels guilty for suspecting dishonorable intentions of such a "capital fellow."

Intending to be cordial, Levin with Vassenka and Stiva sets off for a two-day shooting expedition. Through Vassenka's heedlessness, many small reversals occur throughout the outing. Veslovsky's bungling prevents Levin from a successful catch of snipe. Nevertheless, Levin overcomes his hostility and concludes that, after all, Vassenka is simple, good-hearted, and congenial.

At home once more, Levin's jealousy flares up again. Kitty, as well, is made miserable by Vassenka's attentions. Despite acknowledging his guest's basic guiltlessness, Levin asks Veslovsky to leave. Everyone finds this ridiculous; Levin has no right to indulge his hypersensitivity to needlessly insult a guest. But Kitty and Levin are much relieved to be rid of Vassenka's bumbling presence.

Commentary

This petty incident lasts for ten chapters, although one is devoted to a discussion of economics among the three sportsmen. Innocent and bungling though he is, Vassenka has just been with Anna and Vronsky and, being naive and impressionable, has carried some attitudes from one host's house to the other. Thus the relationship between Anna and Vronsky has polluted the purity of Levin's home; Vassenka has become the "worm in the Garden of Eden." Newly married, Levin and Kitty are particularly sensitive to the narrow bounds between lawful and unlawful love. Their irritability on this point shows, not only the depth and intensity of their own love, but an implicit sense of guilt they feel being so happy together. Their attitude implies that married love is too transient and delicate a matter for basing one's life upon it. This foreshadows the moment when Levin finds supreme solace in religion rather than in sensual and material happiness.

Petty and insignificant though the situation may be, Tolstoy uses it as a vehicle — unconsciously or not — to suggest his own strict views of marital conduct. Later in life, especially in the story *The Kreutzer Sonata,* Tolstoy affirms the extreme position that sexual relations between men and women are basically evil. Levin, who considers Kitty "sacred" while she is pregnant, reflects Tolstoy's potential puritanism and rejection of profane love. Vassenka, on the other hand, superficial and unselfconscious, would be willing to effect a liaison with Kitty were she disposed. Usually sympathetic and compassionate towards Anna, Tolstoy here asserts his moralistic viewpoint as he presents, through Vassenka, the possibility — in parody — for another Anna-Vronsky affair.

CHAPTERS 16 to 25

Summary

Dolly keeps her promise to pay Anna a visit. Driving along, she ponders on the problems of married life. She sighs, considering her whole existence is spent either being pregnant or nursing babies, caring always for children and sometimes losing one despite the cares and worries. She wonders why is everyone so against Anna? Anna has someone who loves her, whereas she (Dolly) has a husband who loves others. Thinking of her life if it included a love affair, all sorts of passionate, impossible romances appear to her fancy. "Anna did quite right," Dolly concludes, "at least she is happy and is making another person happy. I certainly have no reproaches for her."

As her carriage approaches the manor house on Vronsky's estate, Dolly meets Anna on horseback with Veslovsky, Sviazhsky, the Princess Varvara (Anna's aunt), and Vronsky. Anna's face lights up as she recognizes Dolly, and Vronsky warmly greets her. Dolly finds everything about Anna brightened by her love; she is now more beautiful than ever.

Admiring the estate, Dolly is impressed by many new buildings. Those are the servants' cottages, Anna explains. She points out the stud farm, the stables, the new park, and "Alexey's newest passion," a brand new, partly constructed hospital Vronsky built for his peasants. Anna brings Dolly into the well appointed nursery, furnished with modern and expensive

English goods. Impressed by the healthy dark-haired little Ani, Dolly remarks how well she crawls, how pretty she looks.

We always have visitors, Anna says. Men need recreation and Alexey needs an audience. "I must make it lively here or Alexey will look for something fresh. That is why I like all this company," explains Anna, partly to apologize for her free-loading aunt, Princess Varvara Oblonsky. When Dolly calls on the old lady, the Princess says she is here to stand by her niece now that everyone else has thrown Anna over. "They live like the best of married couples," says the aunt, "it is for God to judge them, not for us."

Anna suggests a walk before dinner to show Dolly around the estate. Finding herself with Vronsky, Dolly feels ill at ease for she has never liked his proud manners. But as he enthusiastically explains about his building plans, their architectural design, his intentions for the new hospital, Dolly begins to warm toward him and understands the qualities Anna loves. Drawing her out of earshot of their friends, Vronsky begs Dolly to use her influence and persuade Anna to obtain a divorce. We have one child now, he says, and might have others. Yet they legally belong to Karenin: "unless she can obtain a divorce, the children of the woman I love, will belong to someone who hates them and will have nothing to do with them." Deeply moved, Dolly promises to talk to Anna.

Dinner is elegant and well-prepared; Vronsky is responsible for the excellent choice of food and wine. Anna appears in the third gown Dolly has seen her in that day, while Dolly feels ashamed to wear the one good frock she brought along, and that already patched. She is disturbed at the flirtatious exchanges between Anna and Veslovsky, which Vronsky seems to enjoy. Dolly recalls how Levin dismissed Vassenka for the same behavior. The impersonal atmosphere of this everyday, yet elegant, dinner makes Dolly uncomfortable. Her feelings intensify during the after dinner game of lawn tennis which to her has the "unnaturalness of grown-up people playing a child's game in the absence of children." In this idle atmosphere she suddenly misses the maternal cares and worries after only a one day holiday from them.

While Dolly prepares for bed, Anna comes to her for a private talk. She asks what Dolly thinks of her life. Though looking forward to the end of summer when she and Vronsky will be alone together, Anna says everything shows that "he will spend half his time away from home." Dolly advises divorce so Anna and Vronsky can marry and legitimize Ani and future children. When Anna firmly declares "there will be no more children" because she wishes it so, an unheard-of world presents itself to Dolly for the first time. My only ties to Alexey are those of love, continues Anna, and she must always be fresh and lovely to keep his interest. Dolly feels an impassable gulf of questions separate her from Anna, questions they can never agree on and which remain better unspoken.

Divorce would mean she permanently loses Seriozha, Anna explains to Dolly. Loving her son and her lover equally, "but both more than myself," she continues, is an impossible dilemma. "I cannot have them both, and that's the only thing I want...Nothing else matters," Anna concludes.

Filled with pity for Anna's suffering, Dolly sees her own life with renewed charm. She is eager to go home the next morning, while Anna is sad to see her go. She realizes that with Dolly's departure the feelings aroused in her will never be stirred again.

Commentary

The comparison between Dolly and Anna in this section shows the judgment of Tolstoy the moralist who finds a woman's happiness and source of fulfillment is through raising children. He portrays Anna in her luxurious idleness as if she is one of the guests at Vronsky's estate. Implying she is kept as a high class courtesan where everything is arranged according to Vronsky's tastes and interests, Tolstoy shows that even in daily life Vronsky does not include Anna as an integral part of his career. Confronting Anna's insecurity and suffering, Dolly finds her own routine life with her unloving husband preferable to Anna's life of frivolity. Dolly is also shocked that Anna denies the birth of future children. Her wonderment expresses for Tolstoy the decadence and immorality of Anna's relationship with Vronsky

Yet this is what Vronsky demands, although he is unaware of it. Considering himself as a resolute family man, Vronsky tells Dolly he would like to marry Anna and legitimize his children. But Anna is aware he would become bored with her if she became a housewife like Dolly: Dolly is very nice, says Vronsky, but "too much *terre á terre.*" With this understanding, Anna must remain attractive, avoid pregnancy, and live only for her lover. Though she is honored as a married woman, her position is yet that of a courtesan. The hopeless dilemma is complicated by her inability to choose between Seriozha and Vronsky. Since nothing else matters unless she can have them both, Anna can recklessly live a day by day existence. Her new habit of flirting is a guilt acknowledging gesture which exercises the charm that ties her to Vronsky. Tolstoy thus shows how Anna is already on the road to self-destruction. Dolly's departure, representing Anna's leavetaking of her virtuous past, shows her further commitment to the course of decadence and eventual suicide.

CHAPTERS 26 to 32

Summary
Vronsky and Anna live on in the same way and have much to occupy them. Besides reading many novels, Anna studies in architectural and agricultural journals to keep up with Vronsky's interests. Her knowledge and her memory amaze him, and he frequently discusses problems with her and finds her suggestions helpful. Appreciating all she does out of love for him, he nevertheless chafes at the loving snares she holds him in. Were it not for having scenes each time he attends a civic meeting or a race, Vronsky's chosen career as a progressive landowner would satisfy him entirely.

In October occur the nobility elections in the Kashin province where Vronsky's, Sviazhsky's, Koznyshev's, Oblonsky's, and some of Levin's estates are located. Vronsky is amazed how calmly Anna takes the news of his departure. Not daring to question her deeper responses, he leaves for the elections as a gesture of independence and to allay his boredom.

Since September, Levin and Kitty live in Moscow awaiting her confinement. Bored in the city, Levin agrees to accompany Koznyshev to the Kashin elections. This election is particularly important, Koznyshev explains, for the province marshal exercises tremendous power over education, use of public funds, and appointments of trusteeships. It is now necessary to elect a young, up-to-date progressive marshal to further provincial self-government. Kashin, wealthy and in the vanguard of progress, might serve as a model for other provinces to copy.

Levin does not understand the political power wrangles among the noblemen gathered at the assembly, nor does he attach much importance to the debates, speeches, or voting. He is glad to meet the old landowner he met last year at Sviazhsky's and their conversation expresses what Levin's friends would call a reactionary viewpoint. As the two talk of their loyalty to their farms, despite low profit and much work, Levin recognizes that he and this old landowner represent an ancient tradition of land owning that newcomers, like Vronsky, are changing by turning agriculture into an industry. Levin and his friend work more for love than for capital gain.

Sviazhsky draws Levin toward their group of victorious liberals. Unable to avoid meeting Vronsky, Levin speaks to him with unconscious animosity and tactlessness, displaying his total ignorance of the election proceedings. Vronsky is the host of the victorious election party. He has become so interested in provincial politics, and has actively participated in advancing the winning candidate. He even thinks he might run for office himself at the next election. In this happy frame of mind, Vronsky receives a note from Anna, explaining their daughter is ill with pneumonia and she is very worried. Bitterly, Vronsky contrasts the innocent election festivities with the "sombre burdensome love" to which he must return.

Anna has had no peace of mind since Vronsky left her so coldly. She knows he will be displeased to be asked to return home, and Ani is no longer seriously ill. As usual when Vronsky demands his rights to freedom, Anna concludes with the sense of her own humiliation. "He can go where he pleases, while I can not," she thinks. His cold look shows his love is cooling, but even so, their relationship can never change. Only her love and charm can hold him. She quiets these thoughts with morphine each night so she can sleep. Only marriage will guarantee Vronsky's felicity, Anna decides, and writes Karenin for a divorce. Toward November, they move to Moscow and set up house like a married couple. Each day they expect a reply from Karenin, then a divorce.

Commentary
Even while Anna becomes a worthy helpmeet for Vronsky, advancing his interests with her own efforts, he still feels his freedom restricted. His desire to be responsible only to himself, not to her, reflects his basic irresponsibility.

The election proceedings, seen as frivolous through Levin's eyes, underscore Tolstoy's anarchic demand that human beings must seek personal meaning first. Working for the public good is merely an avoidance on the part of political adepts like Koznyshev to face the basic problem of self-fulfillment.

PART 7

CHAPTERS 1 to 12

Summary
Kitty's delivery is long overdue and Levin, despite himself, settles into the expensive routine of Moscow life. He attends concerts, receives and returns pointless social calls, attends the English Club to dine, drink, and even plays some of the idle games his set indulges in. The club atmosphere of luxury, peace, and conviviality makes him even feel friendly toward Vronsky.

Oblonsky convinces Levin to meet his sister Anna who would be glad to see him. Her position is a trying one, Stiva tells him in the carriage, for none of Anna's women friends call on her. Despite her loneliness, she keeps herself occupied. Besides writing a promising children's book, Anna is taking charge of the destitute dependents of Vronsky's English groom who has ruined himself through drink. She is coaching the boy for school and has taken the girl into her house.

Levin's introduction to Anna is through the portrait he sees in the study. He is charmed by the picture of a woman of almost perfect beauty. Seeing Anna, he realizes the artist had caught her qualities, but finds the reality fresher and more seductive, though less dazzling.

Completely won over by Anna, Levin is touched not only by her charm and cultivation and intelligence, but by her deep sincerity.

When he returns home, Kitty flares up in jealousy noting the "peculiar brilliance of his eyes" from his visit with Anna. Kitty says Anna has bewitched him, that he has fallen in love with her. They become finally reconciled after a long talk.

Home alone, Anna wonders how she cannot refrain from wielding her charms on even a married man in love with his wife. The only one unaffected by her seems to be Vronsky and she blames him for lack of sympathy with her suffering. Vronsky returns home late, happy and cheerful from an evening at the club. His face becomes cold and set when Anna scolds him. She tells him she is "near disaster" when he acts so coldly. Alarmed, Vronsky becomes tender but seems to resent the surrender.

Commentary

Anna's "bewitchment" of Levin is further evidence of her perdition and ultimate doom. Confronting Vronsky's coldness, she feels that "side by side with the love that bound them there had grown up some evil spirit of discord" which neither will be able to overcome.

Levin's sympathy for Anna underlines their similar natures, for each seeks a deeper life meaning than that defined by their social milieu. Tolstoy seems to imply that they might have become lovers under different circumstances. But after this brief coincidence of their parallel careers, Levin and Anna pursue different paths. Hers ends in death while Levin discovers the key to life.

CHAPTERS 13 to 22

Summary

Early one morning, Kitty wakes her husband to inform Levin that the birth pangs have begun. Panicked, Levin rushes to the doctor, to the pharmacist and wonders why everything seems to move with unbearable slowness while Kitty's life is in danger. Later that evening, his son is born. He is awestruck at the strange way of life of women, seemingly so superior and important to that of men. He feels a sense of apprehension at his son – at this new helpless life coming from nowhere that suddenly asserts itself as part of humanity.

Oblonsky, finding his affairs in a bad way, seeks a more lucrative post. He goes to Petersburg to connect with influential people, especially his brother-in-law Karenin. He intends to speak with Alexey Alexandrovitch about Anna as well as about a new position. When Stiva brings up the matter of divorce, Karenin says he will seek "guidance" and give a final answer in two days. On his way out, Stiva visits with Seriozha. He asks if the child remembers his mother. Blushing, the boy murmurs "No," and leaves the room. Mention of his mother has aroused painful memories which Seriozha always tries to repress.

At one of the parties Stiva attends at Betsy Tverskoy's he learns that Karenin is not only influenced by "that half-witted Lydia Ivanovna" but by a "mystic nobody" named Landau who has been so taken up in Petersburg society that one woman has adopted him as her son. Karenin and the countess do not take a step without seeking the advice of this charlatan. Oblonsky calls on the Countess Lydia Ivanovna to ask her to recommend him among her influential friends. There he meets Karenin and Landau, the mystic. The countess and Alexey Alexandrovitch talk only about their new faith which they assure Stiva is the Sacred Truth. Then Landau goes into a trance, and from this state requests Oblonsky to depart. Stiva receives a note from Karenin the next day, a flat refusal for divorce. He realizes this decision is based on what the Frenchman said in his real or sham trance.

Commentary

Levin's mystical wonderment at the birth of his child and women's destiny contrasts ironically with Karenin's mysticism. Levin is on the way to self-realization while Karenin is at a spiritual decline. His new found religious adherence is a way for him to avoid the pain of his humiliation and to save face. Allowing himself to be guided by the ridiculous mysticism of Landau and by the countess' excessive religiosity Karenin no longer assumes personal responsibility. This new belief offers him an even better way to avoid self-confrontation than that offered by his bureaucratic position.

CHAPTERS 23 to 31

Summary

In the suspended condition of awaiting divorce, Anna and Vronsky find their relationship at a standstill. Both are irritable with each other: Anna feels his love is cooling, Vronsky is reproachful that instead of her trying to ease this position he placed himself in for her sake, Anna makes it harder to bear. Without discussing their problem, each seizes every opportunity to prove the other one wrong. Faced with his declining love, Anna assumes his affections belong to someone else. Her jealousy makes her quarrelsome although Vronsky remains faithful. Despite the bitterness, they enjoy brief moments of tenderness.

Their last quarrel begins when Vronsky puts off their journey back to the country because he must see his mother about some property. Anna refuses to let him go, assuming Vronsky wants to visit the attractive Princess Sorokin who lives with the old countess. "You will be sorry for this," she threatens as Vronsky steps into the carriage. Immediately regretful, Anna dispatches a servant with a note begging Vronsky to come back and talk things over. When the note misses him, she writes a telegram to him at his mother's home, and the suspense of waiting makes her desperate. Anna decides to seek Dolly for comfort and advice. Her thoughts during the drive are bitter and distracted. What a dreary business love is, she thinks. She has lost Seriozha and now Vronsky.

Dolly's hall porter informs Anna that Kitty is here, and she is immediately jealous of Vronsky's former love. Unwilling to meet her at first, Kitty's hostility vanishes when she sees "Anna's dear lovely face" again. The three women chat about the baby until Anna, rising, announces she has come to say good-bye, for they are to leave Moscow soon. Smiling, Anna expresses gladness at having seen Kitty again, she has heard so much about her, even from her husband. "He came to see me and I liked him very much," adds Anna with obvious ill intent. Dolly later remarks she has never seen Anna in "such a strange and irritable mood."

Feeling worse than before, conscious of "having been affronted and rejected" by Kitty, Anna feels that all human relationships are based on hate. At home, she reads a telegram from Vronsky: "I cannot return before ten," She would try to meet him at the railway station, she decides; if he is not there, she would go to his country home. In consequence of the scene there, she vaguely considers, she would take the train along the Nizhny line and stop at the first town she comes to. On the way to the station, her impressions crowd her mind — Kitty, Vronsky's cooled passions, her son. First we were irresistibly drawn together, and now we are irresistibly drawn apart, she thinks. My love grows more passionate and selfish while his is dying. It is not jealousy that makes me hateful but my unsatisfaction. As I demand that he give himself entirely up to me, he wants to get further and further from me. I know he is always faithful, but I want his love, not his kindness inspired by a sense of duty. That is much worse than having him hate me. Where love dies, hate begins. Anna glances at the houses she passes, where live people and "more people, and all hating each other." Would things change if she gained her divorce, Anna wonders, and concludes "No." That would not bring them happiness, just "absence of torment." I cause his unhappiness and he mine, she thinks. "Life is sundering us." Love is transient, but hate is everywhere. She loved Seriozha, but exchanged him for another love and did not complain while this other love satisfied her.

Alighting at the station, Anna takes her place in the corner of the train to avoid other people. A porter brings a note from Vronsky saying he is "very sorry" to miss her note but will return at ten. "No, I won't let you torture me," Anna thinks, her words addressed not to Vronsky but to the "powers that made her suffer." At the next station she walks to the edge of the platform in a daze. As a freight train approaches, Anna ducks her head and hurls herself directly under the wheels of the second car. "And the candle by which she had been reading the book filled with trouble and deceit, sorrow and evil, flared up with a brighter light, illuminating for her everything that before had been enshrouded in darkness, flickered, grew dim, and went out forever."

Commentary

As Anna, in her long soliloquy, traces the career which drives her to suicide, she reaches the same conclusion that Tolstoy mentions in *My Confessions*. "It is possible to live only as long as life intoxicates us;" he writes, "as soon as we are sober again we see that it is all a delusion, a stupid delusion." "Love" is the implicit idea in the term "life intoxication;" when Anna finds her love turned to hate, her life becomes a "stupid delusion" and death provides the only alternative. As spontaneously and naturally as Anna once confronted her love, she now accepts death. Always accepting full responsibility for her actions, Anna's suicide is an affirmation of her deep commitment to life. That death is the final truth of her career is expressed by Tolstoy's analogy of Anna's lighted candle which illuminates her life even while she extinguishes the light.

PART 8

CHAPTERS 1 to 5

Summary
Having recently published a book which was poorly received by the public, Koznyshev devotes his energies to promote the cause of the Serbian War which engages the sympathy of the slavophilic newspapers and the entire nation. After working for this cause throughout the spring and summer, he looks forward to a fortnight's rest at his brother's country estate. Koznyshev and his friend Katavasov take a train almost entirely occupied by a load of volunteers on their way to the front. Vronsky and his mother are at the station. Famous not only for his terrible misfortune of two months ago, the Count is known for volunteering himself and a whole squadron which he personally outfitted for the Serbian War. Chatting with Oblonsky, Koznyshev then goes to greet the Countess Vronsky. She describes her son's condition after Anna's death, how he would not speak for six weeks, and only accepted food when she forced him to eat. Begging him to speak with Vronsky, she says he is still miserable and suffers from a toothache as well.

Koznyshev feels dutybound to acclaim Vronsky for what he is doing for the sake of "all Slavic peoples." Lined with suffering, Vronsky's face has aged and his expression is of stone. Since my life is loathsome to me and useless, he tells Koznyshev, I am willing to waste it in this way as in any other. An approaching switch engine reminds him of his pain, and he tries to recall his best moments with Anna. Memories of his cruel and vindictive love poison his recollections. He can clearly picture the mangled body, with her beautiful head still intact, and the expression on her face as if she repeated that dreadful threat—that he would be sorry—she had uttered in their last quarrel. His face distorted by sobs, Vronsky turns from Koznyshev until he masters himself. At the ringing of the bell, they take their respective places on the train.

Commentary
Fiercely pacifist during the sentimental pan-Slavic fervor which brought Russia into the Serbian war against the Turks, Tolstoy's anti-war views implicitly undercut Vronsky's heroism and self-sacrifice. Thus we see Vronsky's gesture is another surrender to impulses which are basically frivolous. When he explains this is as good a way as any other to waste his useless life, Vronsky admits his self-indulgence. The incident underscores his limited morality. Vronsky thus disappears from the novel, hopelessly seeking a goal in life to replace the void left by Anna's death.

But his pilgrimage is doomed to fail. Finding an excuse in the war gives him a chance to avoid the basic confrontation with death, a confrontation which would be his means of salvation.

CHAPTERS 6 to 19

Summary

Nursing the baby, Kitty reflects on her husband's unceasing search for belief. Since the death of his brother, Levin examined the questions of life and death through reading philosophy and through modern scientific concepts which replaced the religious faith of his childhood. Though these ideas are intellectually interesting, Levin thinks, they provide no guidance for life. Feeling like a man "unprepared for life who must inevitably perish because of it." Levin reads tirelessly, but still finds no explanation. "Without knowing what I am and why I am here, life's impossible," he thinks. If I am just a little "bubble-organism" in the immensity of time and space which lasts a little and then bursts, then life is not just a lie, but the "cruel jest of some evil, hateful power to whom one could not submit." Death is the one way to escape this power, and Levin hides gun and rope for fear of committing suicide.

But he exists happily, he discovers, when he ceases worrying about the meaning of life. Absorbed among the thousand daily tasks of his existence—farming, livestock, his family, his hobbies and shooting and bee-keeping—Levin finds satisfaction, but he does not know why.

On an especially busy day, Levin chats with one of his peasants. Remarking on the differences among people, the old man explains why some extend credit and why other don't. "Some men live for their own wants, nothing else," he says, "while some like Fokanitch (an upright old peasant) live for their soul. He does not forget God." Suddenly inspired, Levin asks how one lives "for his soul?" "Why that's plain enough," answers the worker, "It's living rightly, in God's way. Like yourself, for instance. You wouldn't wrong a man..." Feeling wonderfully illuminated, Levin finds the ideas he struggles with so clear they "blind him with their light." And he has been solving the problem of life's significance all along without having realized it, he thinks. One must live with "the greatest goodness possible," and reason and intellect have merely obscured this simple, natural, irrational truth. In light of the truth of "natural goodness" Levin finds everything clear and simple. He returns home with a joyful heart.

While Kitty, the nurse, and the baby are still walking in the woods, Levin gets drawn, against his will, into an argument with Koznyshev and

Katavasov about the Serbian war. Levin believes that a man would sacrifice himself for the sake of his soul, but not for murder. He does not agree that Russia's entry into the war expresses the "will of the people," since a common peasant, for instance, is interested in his immediate material needs. Changing the subject, Levin observes the gathering storm clouds and suggests they all seek shelter.

At the height of the storm, Levin struggles through the forest to search for Kitty and the baby. He finds them drenched, but safe. Fear and relief having torn him from the world of sophistic argument, Levin feels restored by nature and this atmosphere of family love now that the thundershower has passed.

As he and Kitty stand on the terrace, gazing into the clear night sky, Levin feels at peace. My life will still be the same despite my new realization, he thinks. He will still quarrel with Kitty, scold the coachman, express himself tactlessly, and feel remorse afterwards. Though I am still unable to understand with my reason why I pray, he thinks, I will go on praying. But my life is no longer meaningless as it was before. Now "it has the positive meaning of goodness which I have the power to put into it."

Commentary

Book 8 can be considered, on one level, as Tolstoy's polemic against the Russo-Turkish war which broke out in April, 1877 while he was completing the novel. The author's view was so unpopular at the time that Tolstoy's publisher refused to accept the manuscript even though its tone was softened in two successive versions. Levin expresses Tolstoy's pacifist views, based on the idea that the "general welfare" can be achieved only by the strict observance of "the law of right and wrong which has been revealed to every man." The argument with Koznyshev convinces Levin he must pursue his own moral code despite the views of knowledgeable intellectuals. The imminent thunderstorm—an act of nature—turns his thought from these irritating transient matters to his more meaningful concentration on his family. As a literary device, the storm clears Levin's thoughts, while the same storm—that of the war—is merely a vehicle whereby the other characters avoid self-scrutiny and submerge their individual life quests by repeating of cliches like "fighting for freedom," "brotherhood of all Slavs," "national honor," and "upholding Christian faith."

Though *Anna Karenina* concludes with Levin's salvation, Tolstoy has raised many problems he leaves unanswered, and characters who must still confront unresolved lives. Vronsky is embarked on a course of atonement whose end is uncertain, Karenin remains a pitiable cuckold, and Levin, newly inspired by a love of God, remains at the beginning of a long and difficult career.

ANALYSIS OF PLOT
STRUCTURE AND TECHNIQUE

In the middle of his work on *Anna Karenina,* Tolstoy experienced his own moral "conversion" just as Levin does at the novel's conclusion. This was the time when Russia's greatest artist begins to despise art for being an idle, voluptuous, immoral luxury; where Tolstoy discovered life's significance must be self-denying so that one lives "for one's soul" by loving others in the image of God.

With these anti-art commitments, *Anna Karenina* became a tiresome, repellent work for the author. The novel may never have been completed at all were it not that its serialized publication obliged Tolstoy to fulfill his contract with the publisher. Levin reflects Tolstoy's own moral struggle and the novel progresses according to its author's evolving philosophy.

A. Parallel plot

The complexity and sweep of *Anna Karenina* derives from Tolstoy's use of the double plot. While Anna is the central symbolic figure of the story, Konstantin Levin is its hero. Anna and those around her derive their life experience from the highly developed standards of urban civilization, while Levin is a product of the less rigid, individualistic circumstances that obtain in the country. His values derive from his deep-rooted attachment to his ancestral property, while Anna's depend upon her social role as a high society matron. Despite their opposite backgrounds, both protagonists seek a deeper meaning for life beyond the socially defined restrictions of contemporary society. Primarily, Anna and Levin seek love as their basic fulfillment.

Through the vehicle of their parallel careers, Tolstoy seeks to relate and contrast the opposing values of urban life and country life. This dualism lies at the center of his art. For him, the distinction between city life and life on the land represents the fundamental tension between good and evil, between "the unnatural and inhuman code of urbanity" and the "golden age of pastoral life" (quoting Steiner). Developing *Anna Karenina* in terms of this duality, Tolstoy investigates two planes of human experience: the personal and the cultural. This allows him not only to provide insight into the day by day experiences of human beings, but to present a panorama of Russian life at that time.

B. *Anna Karenina as epic*

Despite the basic structure of a multiple plot, *Anna Karenina* is essentially amorphous, lacking what Henry James called a "deep-breathing economy of organic form." Considering, then, the novel as epic prose, we must analyze its temper by contrasting Tolstoy with Homer, rather than his contemporaries like Flaubert or James.

Tolstoy's pagan spirit — his sensual immediacy, his primitive attachment to nature — reflects the Homeric more than the Christian spirit. He himself stated the comparison, remarking of his first works, *Childhood, Boyhood, Youth,* "Modesty aside, they are something like the *Iliad."* Tolstoyan and Homeric epic have these characteristics in common, writes Steiner:

"the primacy of the senses and of physical gesture; the recognition that energy and aliveness are, of themselves, holy; the acceptance of a chain of being extending from brute matter to the stars and along which men have their apportioned places; deepest of all, an essential sanity... rather than those dark obliquities in which a genius of a Dostoevsky was most thoroughly at home."

As an epic intrudes "alien materials" among the main themes without disturbing the artistic equilibrium, *Anna Karenina* embraces excess details, ignoring novelistic form where particulars must all ramify into the main theme. "All things live their own life" in the epic, creating the "proper 'finish' and roundedness out of their own integral significance," writes Steiner. *Anna Karenina* provides many examples of this epic technique. Vividly describing Laska, Levin's pointer, Tolstoy shows an uncanny insight into a dog's experience. The detailed childbirth scene, his sensual awareness of Anna's "beautiful ring-adorned hands," the sympathetic narrative of Seriozha's daydreams, all testify to this voracious appetite for sensual experience — his "genuine epic temper" in other words. Minor characters also live independently, as do minor characters of Homer. Though Karenin's steward, Korney, for example, appears briefly, we sense he has a past and future as much as his master has. This reverence of life for its own sake, not for the sake of the novel, drives Tolstoy to describe with pagan matter-of-factness whenever his characters dine, sweat, bathe, or think sublime thoughts. These epic qualities generate the power of Tolstoyan novels, allowing them to elude the structural bounds which distinguish the "artistically successful" novel from the more imperfect one.

"The truth is we are not to take *Anna Karenina* as a work of art," Matthew Arnold concluded in a criticism; "we are to take it as a piece of life…and what his novel in this way loses in art it gains in reality." Tolstoyan epic, basically a reflection of life, seems a titanic re-creation of life that stands by itself.

C. Technical devices

What inspires literary historians to classify *Anna Karenina* as a psychological novel is Tolstoy's use of "interior monologue." Each major character, through self-discourse, exposes his inner life by recapitulating his motivations, his previous experiences, his plans for future action. The interior monologue gives verbal definition to the semi-articulate processes of a character's consciousness. Anna's soliloquy as she drives to the place of her suicide is an example of this dramatic device.

By his use of stock epithets and recurrent phrases Tolstoy enables us to distinguish among the confusing number of characters. Anna's "dark curls" and "light step" appear frequently. Stiva's "handsome, ruddy face," Kitty's "truthful eyes," and Karenin's "deliberate, high-pitched voice" provide a few examples of this device. These verbal motifs not only suggest points of association, but provide us with indelible impressions of each person's appearance and character.

Tolstoy uses many symbolic devices throughout the novel, too many to enumerate. A partial list follows: the storm corresponding to the stormy state of one's soul; the symbolic value of the train station; the horse race as a working model of the Anna-Vronsky affair; the symbolism of the ball and the theater; Anna's "drooping eyelids" as the first sign of her witchery; her symbolic state of having a "double soul;" the "little man" of death in Anna's dream which echoes the ill-omened railway accident.

Watch for other symbols as you read. Use the Notes' analysis for a guide as you read the book. Notes are a supplement, not a substitute for the book. The Notes are an aid in the same way that an instructor's lectures are intended to enrich your viewpoint.

ANALYSIS OF THEMES

THEMES

A. Marriage

Containing a discussion of at least three marriages, rather than just one as in *Madame Bovary, Anna Karenina* provides an authoritative and thorough, if not definitive, treatment of the subject.

Stiva's relationship with Dolly suggests the incomplete relationship between Karenin and Anna. The Oblonskys' problems only seem lighter because of the double standard: it is less serious for a husband to stray than for a wife, since family unity depends on the woman. Tolstoy shows us that men's primary interests are outside the home, whereas women, like Dolly, center their existence on the family. Stiva, Vronsky, and Karenin, unlike Levin, divide their lives sharply between their homes and amusements, and they are each startled, through the incidents of the novel, to confront the previously ignored feelings of their wives. The divided pattern of these marriages, moreover, allows the dissatisfied partner to seek outside filfillment of social, emotional, or sexual needs. Anna exemplifies the divided nature of an unfulfilled spouse: during her bout of fever, she admits her affection for Karenin though another part of her soul desires Vronsky. Without solving these marital problems, Tolstoy develops his characters so they adjust to their incomplete relationships. Dolly dotes on her children, Anna gives Seriozha the love she cannot express toward Karenin (conversely lacking deep affection for her love-child Ani), while the husbands commit themselves either to work (like Karenin) or pleasure (like Stiva and Vronsky).

Tolstoy thus depicts the hopeless marriage patterns in urban society. Despite showing the blissful union of Kitty and Levin, Tolstoy ultimately states that marriage, and other sexually-based relationships, weaken the individual's quest for "immanent goodness." He prefigures this later doctrine as the love between Anna and Vronsky deteriorates and by the lighthearted intrusion of Vassenka Veslovsky.

While Tolstoy wrote *Anna Karenina,* however, he still exulted in the success of his own marriage. The result is that Levin and Kitty have the only mutually complete union of the novel. Their marriage is a fulfillment, not a compromise, because Levin's family represents an integral part of his search for essential reality. His outside interests and his love are vehicles which aid him to discover the truth of inner goodness. Because Levin's life is more meaningful than the succession of superficial interests which comprise the lives of Stiva, Vronsky, Karenin, his marriage is more meaningful.

From Tolstoy's scheme of Levin's salvation, we must conclude that women are secondary and not individuated. Since a woman's happiness derives from her family, then the wife of a soul satisfied husband will find emotional satisfaction. Tolstoy seems to say that if either Dolly or Anna loved Levin, they, too, would find personal significance in their marriage.

B. Historical necessity

Although Tolstoy has provided an exhaustive discussion of historic causality in *War and Peace,* his concept of "historical necessity" informs the destiny of characters in *Anna Karenina.* The term expresses the conditions in which human consciousness operates: "necessity" provides the form, "consciousness" provides the content. This is merely to paraphrase the thesis that history describes the dynamics of personality (or culture) responding to environmental challenge.

"Historical necessity" is illustrated in *Anna Karenina* according to the personal destinies of the main characters as they react to changing circumstances. Anna's adultery, for example, provides the necessity — that is, the structure — in which Anna, Vronsky, Karenin must retrench their values to overcome the crisis they face. How they meet the challenge of their situation generates the dynamics of the story. Levin's "necessity," how to come to terms with death, forces him to evolve a personal philosophy — a "moral consciousness" — in order to fulfill his life demands.

The nature of each one's response to his particular challenge, however, is defined by the heredity, education, environment which limits his nature. These factors explain why Vronsky remains selfish and fails in love, why Anna commits suicide, why Karenin succumbs to Lydia Ivanovna's influence, why Kitty cannot be like Varenka.

Historical necessity, therefore, is merely a verbal construct which helps us to explain the context in which human awareness operates. In *War and Peace* Tolstoy gives special attention to the forces of mass consciousness and cultural change. *Anna Karenina,* on a much more intimate level, illustrates the forces which allow individuals to confront challenges. They must, like Levin, overcome the crisis, compromise through stagnation, like Karenin and Vronsky, or succumb through death, like Anna.

C. Minor themes

The minor themes, as well as the major ones, all stem from Tolstoy's single-minded morality. His controversial anti-war views, expressed in Part 8, became formalized among the doctrines of Tolstoyan Christianity. A Christian's first duty, Tolstoy later stated, is to abstain from living by the work of others and from participating in the organized violence of the state. While all forms of violence are evil, any government compulsion shares this taint, since the individual must be free to follow his own inner goodness, seeking for himself what is right and wrong. These as yet unformalized doctrines motivate Levin's disinterest in the "Slavonic question" and make him challenge why Russian soldiers should murder Turks.

Despite Tolstoy's anarchic morality, he believes that God's judgment operates the sanctions of moral law. The Pauline epigraph which appears at the novel's title page expresses this fatalism: "Vengeance is mine and I shall repay, saith the Lord" (Romans, 12:19). In other words, the good character gains reward, the bad one is punished; Levin achieves salvation, Anna finds death. Only God judges, not men, says Tolstoy. Depicting the gossiping members of Anna's social set with pitiless irony as they glory in the scandal, Tolstoy chastises these human judges.

ANALYSIS OF MAIN CHARACTERS

KONSTANTIN LEVIN

Levin, on two levels, represents that part of Tolstoy's duality which defines country life as the environment where one may achieve salvation.

On a historic plane, Konstanin Levin speaks for the educated landowners, the backbone of Russian aristocracy in Tolstoy's terms, who defend the traditional national values. If Russia is to discover her modern destiny in an increasingly westernized world, she must depend on individuals like Levin to maintain a core of national identity. Depending from this source of inner strength, the processes of change and progress will effect a cultural enrichment as Russia carries herself firmly through the flux of history.

On a personal level, Levin represents the individual's quest for the meaning of life. This is where Tolstoy autobiographically records Levin's search. Living each moment with great intensity, Levin finds farming, manual work, his relationship with the peasants, a source of satisfaction. He is essentially a realist, not a mystic, and his sense of identity derives from a sensual, tactual communication with the world. Thus we see his feeling of peace after a day's mowing, and his unrest during political meetings. Though his intense nature seeks definition in love, Levin's ideal of family happiness represents, not only immortality, but his quest for roots and substantiality.

Corresponding to his profound hunger for reality, death is his greatest threat. Levin finds death a cruel joke if a life of suffering and struggle suddenly ceases to exist, like that of his brother Nicolai. In order to live at all, Levin discovers, he must come to terms with non-living. Anchored to life by his new family, he begins a head-on confrontation with death. Death is merely part of life, Levin concludes; if one lives "for one's soul" rather than for illusory self-gratification, the end of life is no longer a cruel trick, but a further revelation of life's truths.

What drives home this truth is Levin's sincere belief in God, for God is the source of goodness immanent in everyone's nature. To live without depending on selfish pleasures in order to feel alive, one must act according to this inner goodness. Thus Levin sublimates his selfish demands for love into a generalized love of being, a love of God. The "intoxication with life" which generates his depth and sensitivity, gives way to a "moral intoxication" (to use the term of James T. Farrell). The novel ends on this note of salvation.

ANNA KARENINA

Anna, the other part of Tolstoy's dual scheme, symbolizes the effects of an urban environment on Tolstoy's "natural man." Like Levin, Anna seeks a personal resolution between spontaneous, unreflecting life and the claims of reason and moral law. Being a woman, however, whose human destiny is to raise children and be mistress of her household, Anna is more victimized by culture and society than her male counterpart and is more sensitive to the social restrictions on her quest for personal meaning. Because she is claimed primarily by her position in an advanced — therefore corrupt — society, Anna is doomed at the outset.

Responding only to her inner emotions, she is the most natural character of all the urban noblemen in the novel. The strength of her inner nature enables Anna to cast off from conventional society and seek love as her basic definition.

Tolstoy makes it obvious that Anna's marriage will never satisfy her passionate nature. Karenin, an outstanding example of an individual dehumanized by sophisticated, rational society, is the first one Anna must reject. She must seek the love of a freer, yet honorable, individual. Presenting her with a military man for lover, Tolstoy develops Anna's tragedy with a cruel logical consistency.

Vronsky's brilliant promise in his career implies he has honor, daring, and a sense of life and death any good soldier requires. Opposed to these good qualities is his limited imagination, the military virtues of sacrificing individuality for a sense of corpsmanship, a frivolous attitude toward women, and his rigid code of behavior according to his military standards of "honor" and "prestige." We see the same values that attract Anna to Vronsky provide limitations which doom their liaison to failure. Tolstoy seems to say that Anna's search for love is hopeless: neither Karenin nor Vronsky have the inner power to respond to her emotional intensity. Had Anna fallen in love with Levin, a possibility Tolstoy presents in Part 7, she would have affirmed her love commitment through her children and husband in Levin's country environment.

The specific machinery of Anna's downfall derives from Tolstoy's basic moral philosophy: unselfish seeking of goodness obtains a state of grace, whereas a predatory self-assertion results in damnation. We see how Anna becomes cruel, vindictive, and self-destroying as she exists according to her single goal — to maintain her love relationship. This becomes harder to maintain as Anna loses, one by one, the outside values of the social order which structure not only her existence, but Vronsky's as well. Shut off from her son, her friends, her protective status, Anna's love provides her with the only source of vitality. Under the pressure to live only through her love, she denies her femininity as the vehicle of bearing children; her charms have become the singular weapon of the witch. Thus we see why Vronsky shrinks from her heightened beauty; it is to her witchlike metamorphosis that Vronsky responds so coldly, driving Anna, in her turn, to a state of jealous desperation which further repels him.

Tolstoy shows how Anna, seeking self-gratification in love, drives herself from salvation, away from God, toward satanism and self-destruction. Unlike Levin who had discovered love of God, Anna's search concludes at the dead end of hate, and death is her only recourse.

COUNT VRONSKY

Implying Vronsky's attractiveness as well as his rigidity, Stiva characterizes him as "a perfect specimen of Petersburg's gilded youth." Despite having intense interests — horse racing, politics, his regiment — Vronsky's life depends on various self-gratifications. He has no inner core of identity as Levin has, for his career depends on winning favors from the "powerful in this world." Though he resigns his commission out of what appears to be his principles and pride, he does so merely to pursue a substitute gratification — his passion for Anna. Vronsky's lack of self-scrutiny means he lacks primary self-responsibility; thus he is incapable of responsibility to others. It is his limited depth which sets up his conflict with Anna. Lacking a sense of personal significance, he cannot make his love significant. At the end of the novel, Vronsky, now realizing his guilt at Anna's death, faces a life made tragic by his own limited nature.

ALEXEY KARENIN

Priding himself on his rational, intellectual nature, Karenin symbolizes the very bureaucracy which governs Russia from its capital seat in St. Petersburg. But institutionalized procedure provides no answer to basic life problems. Tolstoy makes this clear when Karenin faces not only his domestic difficulties, but must directly confront the life conditions of Russia's "native tribes." Tolstoy thus symbolizes Karenin on a personal as well as cultural plane.

Becoming humanized with the emotional release he experiences at Anna's deathbed, Karenin has the opportunity to realize himself through love and Christian truths. But in order to adjust to the society that laughs at a cuckold, Karenin reverts to another form of superficial egoism. Perverting his humanizing insights to embrace a hypocritical mysticism, Karenin saves face but loses his personal significance. His new attachment to Countess Lydia Ivanovna symbolizes his pathetic failure.

KITTY SHTCHERBATSKY

Kitty bears a resemblance to Sonya, Tolstoy's wife, and the courtship scene in Part IV is autobiographical. While Kitty's character lacks the interest of Anna's, she is important as an example of a successful woman. Like Karenin, Kitty once embraced a spiritualistic religion to overcome the humiliation of unrequited love, but then came to accept her feminine destiny. Her womanliness, directed at the goals of family happiness, never descends to the witchlike level of Anna's.

Kitty's ill-timed infatuation for Vronsky serves the dramatic function of allowing her to recognize Levin as her true love. Vronsky's rejection at the height of a significant social event allows Kitty to reject the deceit and illusion of town life and follow Levin into the country.

DOLLY OBLONSKY

Although she is a successful woman, in Tolstoyan terms, Dolly fails to retain her husband's love. Compensating this lack by a redoubled interest in the children, Dolly maintains her equilibrium. After her visit to Anna, she is definitively reassured that living like a "hen with her chicks" provides more meaning to life than an existence based on desperate love.

STIVA OBLONSKY

Stiva seems to typify the corruption of human values that Tolstoy blames on city refinements. His "natural goodness" perverted by a life of pleasure seeking, he fails to appreciate his wife's worth and destroys a significant part of her life. His unwitting powers of destruction are echoed in the incident where he is the tool for devaluation of Russia's forest resources.

Stiva shares many qualities with Anna, though they lack the intensity of her quest for emotional commitment. But it is this very lack which makes Stiva a corruptive influence in the nation and in his intimate circle, while Anna's intensity makes her destroy only herself. Like Anna, Stiva responds to emotions, not conventions, while, by contrast to his sister, his superficiality allows him to satisfy his needs within his social environment.

MINOR CHARACTERS

Anna Karenina provides a catalogue of minor characters, each representing many aspects of Tolstoy's thematic duality, the conflict between urban and country based values. There is not space enough to mention the significance we can attach to each one, and a few suggestions have been previously made, especially referring to Koznyshev, Varenka, Vasenka Veslovsky, Nicolai Levin, and Ryabinin.

REVIEW QUESTIONS AND THEME TOPICS

1. Why do Tolstoy's characters have to come to terms with death in order to understand life? (See "General analysis," commentaries in Part 3.)

2. Discuss Tolstoy's philosophy in terms of the "natural life" of the country and the unnatural life of the city. (See "General analysis" and commentaries in Part 3.)

3. Why does Tolstoy attach equal importance to the everyday occurrences of individual life as to large happenings like war, politics, intellectual currents? (See subsection on "historical necessity" in General analysis; mostly though, you must consider your own impressions of the novel itself.)

4. Try to describe Anna's tragedy in your own words. Consider her career if she remained faithful to Karenin and then consider the rewards of her guilty existence with Vronsky. Is there a right and wrong in her choice of destiny? Does Anna have a choice?

5. What is the significance of the scriptural quotation on the novel's title page: "Vengeance is mine and I will repay, saith the lord."? (See General Analysis.)

6. Consider the ironic significance of the following incidents: Anna's attendance at the theater (Part 5); Dolly's renewed attraction to her own life after she visits Anna (Part 6); the contrasting reactions of Levin and Vronsky to Vassenka Veslovsky (Part 6); the reversed roles of lover and husband while Anna lies ill (Part 4.)

7. If you have read *Madame Bovary*, compare Flaubert's treatment of marriage with Tolstoy's in *Anna Karenina*.

8. Discuss the epic qualities of *Anna Karenina* which made Henry James criticize Tolstoyan novels as "loose and baggy monsters." (See General Analysis.)

9. What is significant about Stiva's sale of the forest property to Ryabinin the speculator? (See Commentary in Part 2.)

10. What is the significance of Anna's deathbed scene? (See commentary in Part 4.)

11. What is the significance of the horse race? (See commentary in Part 2.)

12. What significance do the following characters have in the novel: Koznyshev, Varenka, Betsy Tverskoy, Lydia Ivanovna, the old peasant of Part VII.

13. Discuss Anna's power of fascination and her capacity for cruelty that Kitty suspects in Part 1. (See commentaries in Part 1 and elsewhere.)

14. What characteristics do Anna and Levin share?

15. What characteristics do Vronsky and Karenin share?

SELECTED BIBLIOGRAPHY

James T. Farrell, "Introduction to *Anna Karenina*," in *Literature and Morality*. New York: Vanguard Press, 1947.

Thomas Mann, "Goethe and Tolstoy," in *Essays of Three Decades;* New York: Alfred A. Knopf, 1948.

Thomas Mann, "Anna Karenina," in *Essays of Three Decades,* New York: Alfred A. Knopf, 1948.

D. S. Merezhkovsky, *Tolstoy as Man and Artist, with an essay on Dostoevsky;* London: 1902.

Earnest J. Simmons, *Leo Tolstoy,* 2 vols. Vintage Press (paperbound division of Random House.)

George Steiner, *Tolstoy or Dostoievsky, an Essay in the Old Criticism;* New York: Alfred A. Knopf, 1959.

Alexandra Tolstoy, *Tolstoy: A Life of my Father;* trans. by E. R. Hapgood; New York: Harper Brothers, 1953.

NOTES